KAAL SARP DOSHA: Truth, Symptoms & Remedies

Astrology Remedies & Solutions, Volume 4

Dr.Narayanan Namboodiri

Published by G.K.MENON, 2026.

KAAL SARP DOSHA

Truth, Symptoms & Remedies

Series: *Astrology Remedies & Solutions*

Written by

Dr. Narayanan Namboodiri

Published by

P. K. Gopalakrishnan

Disclaimer

This book is intended for **educational and informational purposes only**. The astrological interpretations, spiritual practices, and remedies mentioned in this book are based on **traditional Vedic beliefs** and are not a substitute for professional medical, legal, financial, or psychological advice.

The author and publisher make **no guarantees** regarding results, outcomes, or benefits. Readers are advised to use **personal discretion and judgment** while applying any remedies.

If you have serious health concerns, emotional distress, or legal/financial issues, please consult a qualified professional.

Dedication

Dedicated to those who ask questions.

To those who refuse to accept fear as a conclusion.

To those who examine life patterns with honesty,

and seek remedies that strengthen the mind,

rather than rituals that weaken confidence.

May this work help you separate

what is real from what is exaggerated,

and guide you toward remedies that are

simple, practical, and consistent.

About the Author

Dr. Narayanan Namboodiri is a respected **Vedic Astrologer, Guide, and Mentor**, widely appreciated for his calm, disciplined, and spiritually grounded approach to astrology. As a **PhD Scholar**, he brings together the depth of traditional Vedic knowledge and the clarity of academic research, presenting astrology not merely as prediction, but as a structured system for understanding **karma, timing, responsibility, and human transformation**.

Over the years, Dr. Narayanan Namboodiri has guided many individuals through critical phases of life—career uncertainty, financial instability, relationship struggles, health-related concerns, and periods of intense mental pressure—by interpreting planetary influences with accuracy and practical wisdom. His work is especially recognized for its focus on **Saturn (Shani)**, Rahu–Ketu dynamics, and karmic patterns that shape long-term destiny.

What distinguishes Dr. Narayanan Namboodiri's teachings is his emphasis on **ethical astrology**. He believes that the purpose of astrology is not to create fear, dependency, or superstition, but to provide seekers with **inner clarity, disciplined remedies, and confidence to face life with maturity**. His remedy approach is rooted in classical Vedic tradition and focuses on realistic, meaningful practices such as **discipline, charity, prayer, self-control, and service to society**—the true path through which planetary challenges are transformed into personal strength.

Dr. Narayanan Namboodiri's guidance highlights a powerful truth:

Planets do not punish human beings—planets correct human beings.

In this view, Saturn becomes the great architect of time, shaping character through patience and responsibility; Jupiter becomes the teacher of wisdom and blessings; Venus refines love and harmony; and Rahu–Ketu reveal hidden karmic lessons and spiritual evolution.

Through his books in the **Astrology Remedies & Solutions** series, Dr. Narayanan Namboodiri aims to create a reliable reference for readers who want astrology that is **simple to understand, practical to apply, and spiritually elevating**. His writings are designed for both beginners and serious learners, offering structured explanations, real-life symptom recognition, and step-by-step remedies that can be followed safely and consistently.

His mission is to help people move from confusion to clarity, from fear to faith, and from obstacles to growth—by aligning life with the higher principles of **dharma, discipline, and inner truth**.

P.K.Gopalakrishnan

／
Acknowledgement

This book was shaped by a long process of observation, reflection, and careful questioning.

Kaal Sarp Dosha is often discussed with emotion, fear, and exaggeration—yet the sincere seeker deserves clarity, balance, and practical guidance. This work is an attempt to present the subject with respect for tradition, while maintaining realism, discipline, and intellectual honesty.

I offer my sincere gratitude to all readers and seekers who inspired this work—especially those who approached Jyotisha not as superstition, but as a meaningful system of insight and self-correction. Their questions, struggles, and lived experiences helped form the investigative spirit behind these pages.

I also acknowledge the wisdom preserved through generations of authentic Vedic tradition, and the teachers and practitioners whose disciplined approach reminds us that remedies are not shortcuts, but structured methods to restore inner stability and life direction.

My heartfelt thanks to **P. K. Gopalakrishnan**, the publisher, for supporting this work and enabling its completion.

Finally, I express gratitude to the Divine force that guides every sincere search for truth—

may this book serve as a lamp of clarity for those walking through uncertain shadows.

Dr. Narayanan Namboodiri

Introduction — The Serpent Line in the Sky

There are certain moments in life when a person feels something strange—

not visible, not measurable, yet undeniably present.

You work hard, but results arrive late.

You plan carefully, yet sudden reversals appear.

You rise close to success, then something pulls you back.

And after a point, a silent question begins to repeat inside the mind:

"Why does this keep happening to me?"

In Jyotisha, one of the most powerful answers given to this question is **Kaal Sarp Dosha**—a formation surrounded by mystery, fear, temple rituals, and endless opinions. Some call it a curse. Some deny it completely. Some exploit it as a business. And many sincere people suffer—not because of the dosha alone, but because of the panic created around it.

This book is not written to frighten you.

It is written to **equip you.**

Because Kaal Sarp Dosha is not merely a dramatic label. It is a pattern—an axis—an invisible pressure line in the horoscope where **Rahu and Ketu** form a corridor of intense karmic movement. When the timing is right, that corridor can feel like a storm inside life: delays, confusion, instability, sudden turns, emotional restlessness, and strange cycles that repeat until they are understood.

Yet here is the truth most people never hear:

Kaal Sarp Dosha does not always destroy.

Sometimes, it transforms.

Many powerful individuals—leaders, innovators, spiritual seekers, and survivors—have carried this formation. Their lives were not "easy," but their lives became intense, disciplined, and deeply purposeful. The dosha does not always close doors. Often, it forces the soul to stop wasting energy and begin walking with sharp awareness.

So the real question is not only:

"Do I have Kaal Sarp Dosha?"

The real question is:

"What is it doing in my life right now—and what should I do about it?"

That is what this book investigates.

Inside these chapters, you will find:

- **The truth** behind Kaal Sarp Dosha—without exaggeration
- **Symptoms and life patterns** explained realistically
- **Correct diagnosis methods**, including false positives
- **Practical remedies** that are simple, consistent, and effective
- A path that removes fear and replaces it with **discipline and control**

This book does not demand blind belief.

It invites intelligent observation.

You do not need to become superstitious.

You only need to become **aware.**

Because when you understand the shadow,

it stops controlling you from behind.

And when you apply the right remedies—

not as panic rituals, but as structured correction—

the same "dosha" that once felt like a curse

can become the pressure that shapes your strength.

So let us begin the investigation.

Not to escape destiny,

but to master your response to it.

Part I — The Investigation

Clarity, Structure, and Correct Understanding

Kaal Sarp Dosha is a powerful astrological formation that highlights important karmic patterns and life-direction themes. When understood correctly, it becomes a valuable guide for strengthening stability, improving decision-making, and applying effective remedies with confidence.

This section presents a clear, structured foundation for accurate understanding. It explains how the Rahu–Ketu axis functions, how the formation is identified, and how its intensity is assessed through practical chart principles. The focus is simple: **knowledge first, then solutions.**

With this clarity, the reader gains a strong starting point for meaningful progress and steady transformation.

Chapter Heads (Part I)

1. The Shadow Claim

2. The Real Axis

3. The Formation

4. False Alarms

5. Severity Codes

6. The Trigger Window

Chapter 1 — The Shadow Claim

Separating Myth from Mastery, and Fear from True Understanding

Kaal Sarp Dosha is one of the most spoken names in modern astrology.

It travels through conversations, social media, family advice, and public opinion like a mysterious shadow—often mentioned with intensity, yet rarely explained with precision.

Some call it destiny's obstacle.

Some call it a curse.

Some call it the reason behind every delay, every struggle, every sudden change.

But Jyotisha does not function through exaggeration.

Jyotisha functions through **structure**.

And the very first step in mastering Kaal Sarp Dosha is this:

to recognize the difference between what is claimed and what is true.

This chapter begins the investigation. It clears confusion without creating doubt. It establishes confidence without creating fear. And it opens the reader into the correct way of seeing the Rahu–Ketu corridor—so that the rest of the book becomes not only meaningful, but immediately useful.

Because when truth is clear, remedies become powerful.

And when remedies become powerful, destiny becomes cooperative.

---

1) Why Kaal Sarp Dosha Is Spoken About So Strongly

Kaal Sarp Dosha carries a mystic name.

It carries an intense reputation.

And it carries a unique visual formation in the horoscope that attracts attention immediately.

But the strength of public talk does not always equal the strength of astrological reality.

Kaal Sarp Dosha became widely discussed because it is easy to describe in one sentence:

"All planets are trapped between Rahu and Ketu."

That sentence creates instant emotion.

And emotion spreads faster than understanding.

Yet Jyotisha is not a language of fear.

It is a language of measurement.

So the first responsibility of a serious reader is to approach this formation with the mindset of a researcher—not to deny it, not to dramatize it, but to **understand it correctly.**

---

2) The Shadow Claim: What People Commonly Say

The "shadow claim" is the collection of popular statements that surround Kaal Sarp Dosha. These statements are often repeated, and because they are repeated, they feel powerful.

Common claims include:

- "Nothing will work in life."
- "Success will always be blocked."

- "Marriage will never stabilize."
- "Money will never stay."
- "The person will always suffer."

Such claims may sound dramatic, but they are not professional Jyotisha.

They are emotional interpretations.

A true astrologer does not speak in absolutes.

A true astrologer speaks in **structures, timing, and solutions.**

This book is written in that higher tradition.

---

3) The Investigative Lens: How Jyotisha Reads a Formation

A horoscope is not a single line.

It is a complete system.

In professional Jyotisha, no formation is judged alone. Every formation is studied through:

- the strength of Lagna (Ascendant)
- the condition of Moon (mind stability)
- the dignity of planets involved
- benefic support and protective yogas
- timing through dasha and transit
- the native's discipline and choices

This is the true investigative method.

So the correct question is never:

"Does Kaal Sarp Dosha exist?"

The correct question is:

How is the Rahu–Ketu corridor functioning in this chart, and what is the correct remedy strategy?

That is mastery.

---

4) What Kaal Sarp Dosha Truly Indicates

Kaal Sarp Dosha is not a verdict.

It is a signature.

It indicates that the Rahu–Ketu axis becomes a dominant corridor of experience. It can intensify certain life themes, refine priorities, and accelerate karmic learning through timing.

In simple terms:

- it increases the importance of discipline
- it increases the importance of timing
- it increases the need for mental stability
- it creates a strong transformation corridor
- it rewards consistency with visible results

This is why many natives with this formation become highly capable. Their life may not move casually. But it moves with meaning. And when they learn to stabilize the corridor, they often rise with remarkable strength.

Kaal Sarp Dosha is not a "stop."

It is a **training path.**

---

5) Why the Name Feels Powerful

Names carry vibration.

And the name "Kaal Sarp" naturally creates an intense impression.

"Kaal" suggests time.

"Sarp" suggests a serpent—symbolic of hidden movement, deep transformation, and subtle power.

But the wise reader must understand:

in Jyotisha, symbols are not threats.

Symbols are **messages.**

The serpent is also a guardian in spiritual tradition.

It represents energy that can be dangerous when uncontrolled, and powerful when disciplined.

That is exactly how Rahu–Ketu behaves.

So the name itself is not a warning.

It is a code.

A code that says:

"Master timing. Master discipline. Master the mind."

---

6) The Real Problem: Not the Dosha, But the Disorder

When people struggle under this formation, the root cause is usually not the chart itself. The root cause is often:

- scattered routine
- inconsistent effort
- impulsive decisions
- emotional reaction cycles
- lack of spiritual rhythm

- ignoring timing intelligence

Kaal Sarp Dosha magnifies the results of these patterns.

But the greatest secret is this:

When order enters life, the corridor becomes protective.

This is why the Remedy Vault is so powerful.

It creates order.

And order is the antidote.

---

7) The First Victory: Clarity Without Fear

This chapter's purpose is to give you the first victory:

- not fear
- not doubt
- not confusion

But clarity.

Kaal Sarp Dosha is a formation that can be measured, understood, and stabilized. It responds beautifully to structured remedies. And the seeker who practices consistently gains something greater than temporary relief:

permanent inner command.

When the mind becomes steady, destiny becomes steady.

---

8) The Reader's Power: You Are Not Helpless

This book is written with a realistic approach and practical solutions because the reader must feel empowered. The horoscope is a map, not a prison.

Your effort matters.

Your discipline matters.

Your rhythm matters.

And the Rahu–Ketu corridor respects these three forces more than anything else.

That is why the reader is never helpless.

The moment you begin the correct system, the corridor begins to change.

---

9) Closing Insight: The Shadow Claim Ends Here

The shadow claim is loud.

Truth is silent and strong.

From this point onward, this book will not speak in fear-based exaggerations. It will speak in structured understanding, investigative clarity, and practical methods that can be practiced immediately.

Because the final truth of Chapter 1 is luminous:

Kaal Sarp Dosha is not the end of destiny.

It is the beginning of mastery.

Chapter 2 — The Real Axis

Rahu-Ketu: The Serpent Line That Breathes Through Destiny

There is a presence in the horoscope that does not announce itself like thunder.

It moves like a whisper across time.

It does not demand attention—yet it quietly shapes attention.

It does not force the hand—yet it guides the hand.

In Jyotisha, that presence is known through a single, luminous corridor:

the **Rahu-Ketu axis.**

This axis is not merely a line drawn between two points. It is a **mystic current**—a living pathway where destiny becomes purposeful, where the mind learns through intensity, and where the soul refines itself through deeper awareness. It is called a shadow line not because it is dark, but because it is subtle—like the fragrance of incense that cannot be held, yet fills the entire room.

When Rahu-Ketu becomes strong in a chart, life begins to feel guided by an unseen intelligence. Events align like symbols. Experiences repeat like messages. Turning points arrive like doors opening in silence. The native senses that life is not random—it is arranged.

And this is the first secret of the axis:

it does not create mystery—it reveals order.

Kaal Sarp Dosha is born from this order. It is the axis becoming the central corridor through which the planets move—like stars drawn into a sacred alignment. Therefore, before we study the dosha, we must first understand the axis itself, because the axis is the key that unlocks the entire mechanism.

---

1) The Hidden Geometry of the Shadow

Rahu and Ketu are defined by the lunar nodes—the meeting points where the Moon's path intersects the Sun's path. These are the same points that allow eclipses to occur: moments when light is temporarily veiled, and the sky itself performs a sacred rearrangement.

In Jyotisha, this becomes more than astronomy.

It becomes a spiritual language:

Where light can be covered, consciousness can be transformed.

That is why Rahu and Ketu are called *Chhaya Grahas*—shadow forces. Their power does not depend on visibility. It depends on impact. Their influence moves like a tide beneath the surface, shaping choices, shaping cravings, shaping detachment, shaping the direction of life's unfolding.

The axis is not an object.

It is a **field**.

And within that field, destiny begins to speak.

---

2) One Corridor, Two Gates

Rahu and Ketu stand opposite each other like two ancient guardians at the ends of a sacred corridor. They form one line, yet they open two different worlds.

- **Rahu is the gate of expansion.**
- **Ketu is the gate of refinement.**

Rahu calls the mind outward—toward experience, achievement, ambition, and worldly mastery.

Ketu calls the soul inward—toward silence, clarity, wisdom, and spiritual precision.

Together, they create a rhythm that is unmistakable:

the hunger to rise, and the wisdom to purify.

the desire to conquer, and the ability to detach.

the world that demands effort, and the silence that demands understanding.

When the Rahu–Ketu axis becomes dominant, life develops a certain sacred intensity. Not an intensity of disturbance, but an intensity of meaning. The native begins to recognize that each phase of life carries a lesson, and each lesson carries a key.

This is why the axis is revered:

it does not merely show what happens—

it shows **what is being shaped.**

---

3) Rahu: The Ascending Serpent of Desire and Power

Rahu is the great magnifier.

It enlarges the mind's ambition and sharpens the hunger for expansion. Where Rahu stands, the desire to rise becomes vivid. The mind becomes fascinated by growth, influence, achievement, and the mastery of complex systems.

Rahu does not settle for small outcomes.

It seeks the larger horizon.

Rahu creates a distinctive aura in life:

- bold movement toward results
- rapid learning through experience
- attraction toward innovation and modern pathways
- courage to take unusual routes
- intensity that turns ordinary effort into powerful ambition

In mystic language, Rahu is the serpent that climbs upward—

not with noise, but with unstoppable momentum.

It carries the message:

"Expand beyond your limits."

Rahu is the force that teaches the native how to command the outer world—not through luck, but through strategic growth and disciplined action.

---

4) Ketu: The Serpent of Inner Fire and Silent Mastery

If Rahu expands, Ketu refines.

Ketu is the quiet blade of wisdom. It cuts away unnecessary attachments, not as loss, but as purification. It strengthens the inner core. It draws the native toward depth, precision, and truth.

Where Ketu stands, life becomes sacred.

Not because life becomes distant, but because life becomes essential.

Ketu carries a unique spiritual signature:

- clarity without constant explanation

- inner strength without dependence
- silence that holds intelligence
- detachment that protects the mind
- devotion that deepens the soul

In mystic language, Ketu is the serpent that moves inward—

not to withdraw from life, but to master life from the inside.

It carries the message:

"Refine until only truth remains."

Ketu does not reduce the native's power.

It concentrates it.

---

5) The Axis as a Living Presence in Human Life

When Rahu and Ketu become strong, the native's life begins to reveal patterns that feel almost scripted—yet always meaningful. It is as if the universe is teaching through repeated symbols.

A) The mind becomes destined toward focus

Certain themes become central: career, identity, stability, relationships, purpose, spiritual direction. The native cannot treat these themes casually. They demand attention and reward discipline.

B) Turning points arrive like silent gateways

A door closes. Another opens. A new direction becomes visible. Life chapters form naturally, each one shaping the next with remarkable logic.

C) Lessons repeat until they become skills

The axis teaches through repetition. And repetition is the secret method of mastery. The same lesson returns with greater refinement until the native becomes strong enough to rise beyond it.

This is the mystic nature of Rahu–Ketu:

it shapes life like a teacher shapes a student—

through experience, correction, and growth.

---

6) The Axis as the Clock That Activates Destiny

Rahu–Ketu is not only symbolic. It is also a timing force. It becomes highly active during specific periods—especially through phases and transits connected to the axis.

When those windows open, life begins to move faster, not randomly, but purposefully. The native experiences:

- stronger motivation to correct life direction
- sharper awareness of consequences
- deeper need for stability and discipline
- rapid progress when remedies are consistent

Timing is the sacred clock of Jyotisha.

And Rahu–Ketu is one of its strongest hands.

When timing aligns, the axis becomes a spiritual wind behind the sail.

Effort becomes effective.

Practice becomes powerful.

Remedies become visible in their results.

---

7) The Axis as the Spine of Kaal Sarp Dosha

Kaal Sarp Dosha is the Rahu–Ketu corridor becoming the main highway of the horoscope. When planets fall within this enclosure, the axis becomes the central channel through which life energy flows.

This creates a remarkable life signature:

- concentrated karmic learning
- strong focus on key life themes
- accelerated transformation through discipline
- powerful results through correct remedy alignment

In such charts, the axis is not a side feature.

It becomes the spine of the destiny narrative.

And once the spine is understood, the entire chart begins to reveal its order.

---

8) The Great Revelation: The Axis Trains the Native

The highest function of Jyotisha is not to create emotion.

It is to create mastery.

And the Rahu–Ketu axis is one of its greatest instruments because it reveals where the native can become exceptionally strong through awareness and disciplined practice.

When the axis is understood:

- decisions become clean
- habits become stable
- confidence becomes natural
- progress becomes steady
- remedies become meaningful

The final truth of this chapter is luminous:

Rahu and Ketu do not weaken the native—

they awaken the native.

They do not close the path.

They illuminate the path.

And once illuminated, the seeker walks forward with certainty—

not merely to live, but to evolve.

With this axis now clearly revealed, we are ready for the next step:

to study **how Kaal Sarp Dosha is formed**, and how its structure is identified with precision in the horoscope.

Chapter 3 — The Formation

How Kaal Sarp Dosha Takes Shape Inside the Horoscope

A horoscope is not merely a chart of planets.

It is a sacred arrangement—an architecture of timing, direction, and inner evolution.

When we look at a birth chart with trained eyes, we do not see scattered symbols. We see patterns that behave like living signatures. Some patterns are gentle and supportive. Some are intense and refining. And a few patterns stand out like a powerful seal—quietly announcing that this life carries a concentrated karmic corridor.

Kaal Sarp Dosha is one such formation.

It is called a "dosha" because it indicates a special condition of alignment. Yet its deeper nature is far more elegant: it is a **mystic enclosure**, a structured channel where the Rahu–Ketu axis becomes the main pathway through which the planets express themselves. When this formation exists, the chart does not lose strength—it gains **focus**. It becomes a map of purposeful learning, accelerated maturity, and disciplined transformation.

To understand Kaal Sarp Dosha fully, we must study how it forms—step by step—so the reader gains certainty, clarity, and practical confidence.

---

1) The Corridor of Rahu and Ketu

The Rahu–Ketu axis is like a cosmic line drawn across the sky of the horoscope. It divides the chart into two halves, creating a corridor of experience. In Kaal Sarp Dosha, the planets are positioned in such a way that this corridor becomes the dominant chamber of the chart.

The classical definition is simple in structure:

When all planets fall within the arc between Rahu and Ketu,

the formation becomes complete.

This does not mean life becomes narrow. It means life becomes **directed**. The planetary energies begin to move within a concentrated karmic pathway—like a river that flows through a sacred channel, gathering power as it travels.

In this corridor, life becomes deeply organized around growth. The chart becomes a training ground for mastery, where lessons appear with purpose and progress is built through awareness.

---

2) Why the Formation Feels Powerful

The strength of Kaal Sarp Dosha comes from one central principle:

the entire planetary system becomes conditioned by the axis.

When planets fall within the Rahu–Ketu enclosure, their expression is not scattered across the chart. It is gathered, concentrated, and refined. This produces a distinct signature:

- life themes become highly focused
- experiences feel meaningful and destined
- growth becomes accelerated through timing
- transformation becomes visible through discipline

The native often develops a strong inner seriousness. Decisions matter more. Consequences become clearer. The mind becomes sharper through experience. This is why the formation is remembered: it produces a life that evolves through **structure**, not randomness.

In mystic terms, the formation acts like a seal placed upon the chart, saying:

"This life is designed for transformation."

---

3) The Two Forms: Complete and Partial Enclosure

In professional Jyotisha, Kaal Sarp Dosha is read with precision. The formation may appear in two broad forms:

A) Complete Formation

When all planets fall within the Rahu–Ketu corridor, the axis becomes the main channel of expression. This creates a strong and clear signature of focused life learning.

B) Partial Formation

When most planets fall within the corridor, but one or more planets stand outside, the axis remains influential yet the chart has additional balancing currents. This produces a different rhythm—still intense and meaningful, yet often more diversified in expression.

Both forms are valuable to understand, because the purpose of diagnosis is not labeling—it is selecting the right method of remedies. Precision strengthens results.

---

4) The Role of Houses: Where the Serpent Line Breathes

Kaal Sarp Dosha is not interpreted only by "presence." It is interpreted by **placement.**

The houses occupied by Rahu and Ketu reveal where the karmic corridor becomes most active. Each axis placement produces a distinct life theme, such as:

- identity and self-mastery
- family stability and emotional grounding
- courage and action refinement
- career focus and public responsibility
- relationships and partnership evolution
- spiritual discipline and inner purification

In mystic narrative terms, the axis shows where the serpent energy coils itself most strongly—where destiny insists on maturity, and where the soul gathers power through correction.

This is why two people can have the same formation and still experience it differently:

because the houses determine **where the current flows**.

---

5) The Strength of Rahu and Ketu: The Hidden Quality Test

The formation becomes clearer when the quality of Rahu and Ketu is assessed. A serious reading always examines:

- the sign placement of Rahu and Ketu
- the dignity and support they receive
- conjunctions with benefic or malefic planets
- aspects influencing the axis
- the stability of the Lagna and Moon
- Jupiter's protective influence

This evaluation is essential because Jyotisha is not a single-factor system. It is a complete architecture. The axis is central, yet it operates through the overall strength of the chart.

When Rahu–Ketu is supported well, the formation becomes a powerful engine of progress. The native gains the ability to rise rapidly through disciplined action and inner clarity.

This is one of the most uplifting truths of Jyotisha:

structure becomes strength when supported by correct guidance.

6) The Planetary Story Inside the Corridor

When planets gather within the Rahu–Ketu enclosure, each planet expresses its role through the corridor's rhythm.

- **Sun** expresses authority and identity through karmic refinement
- **Moon** expresses emotions through deeper discipline and clarity
- **Mars** expresses action through strategic focus
- **Mercury** expresses intelligence through sharp decisions
- **Jupiter** expresses wisdom as a guiding lamp within the corridor
- **Venus** expresses relationships through maturity and depth
- **Saturn** expresses responsibility through structured stability

In this formation, planets do not lose their nature. They become more purposeful. Their lessons become clearer. Their results become stronger when the native works with discipline.

This is why the formation can be studied like a manuscript:

each planet is a chapter, and the axis is the binding.

7) Timing: When the Formation Becomes Most Visible

Even when Kaal Sarp Dosha is present, its results become most noticeable during specific timing windows. Jyotisha is always timing-sensitive, and timing is the sacred clock that reveals the active chapter of life.

The formation becomes more pronounced during:

- Rahu and Ketu dashas and sub-periods
- periods connected to the axis houses
- transits that activate Rahu, Ketu, Moon, or Lagna
- life transitions where destiny demands correction and growth

When timing aligns, the corridor becomes luminous. The native experiences faster learning, stronger turning points, and clearer opportunities for transformation. Remedies applied during these windows become highly effective, because timing provides momentum.

This is why this book emphasizes practical solutions:

right method + right timing = visible progress.

---

8) The Essence of the Formation: A Seal of Focus

The deepest meaning of Kaal Sarp Dosha can be expressed in one sentence:

It concentrates the life-path so that growth becomes unmistakable.

This formation is a signature of evolution through focus. It teaches the native to master the mind, refine choices, strengthen discipline, and rise with stability. It turns ordinary life into a purposeful journey where awareness becomes power and consistency becomes protection.

The reader should remember this clearly:

Kaal Sarp Dosha is not a wall.

It is a corridor.

And every corridor leads somewhere.

With the formation now clearly understood, the next chapter becomes natural:

how to confirm it with full precision and how to recognize supportive factors that strengthen the chart's overall balance.

Chapter 4 — False Alarms

The Art of Confirmation: When the Serpent Line Is Read with Precision

In the language of Jyotisha, truth is never hurried.

It is approached like a flame in a temple—

with steadiness, respect, and perfect attention.

Because the horoscope is not a place for confusion.

It is a place for clarity.

Kaal Sarp Dosha is a powerful formation, and power always deserves correct recognition. When a formation is identified with precision, the chart becomes luminous—like a map revealed under sacred light. The reader gains calm confidence, and the remedy path becomes direct, effective, and beautifully practical.

This chapter is devoted to a single purpose:

to establish certainty.

Not through doubt, not through fear, but through professional verification. In Jyotisha, confirmation is not a barrier. It is a blessing. It ensures that every conclusion rests on solid ground, and every remedy becomes meaningful.

---

1) Precision Is the First Remedy

Before any practice begins, the wise reader learns one sacred principle:

accuracy itself is a remedy.

When the mind knows exactly what is present in the chart, it becomes steady. The heart becomes confident. The path becomes clear. Jyotisha becomes what it is meant to be: a science of guidance, a spiritual instrument of order.

Kaal Sarp Dosha is identified by a specific structure. That structure must be confirmed with disciplined observation, because the Rahu–Ketu axis is subtle and powerful, and the horoscope contains many patterns that may appear similar on the surface.

This chapter teaches the reader how to recognize the formation with clean certainty, so that the chart speaks with one voice.

---

2) The Horoscope Has Many Serpent Currents

Rahu and Ketu create strong energetic currents in many charts. Fven withont a complctc Kaal Sarp enclosure, the axis may still feel significant, because the nodes influence desire, focus, timing, and inner transformation.

Tlis ls why the wise practitioner reads with depth:

- some charts show **axis prominencc**
- some charts show **axis dominance**
- some charts show **axis refinement**

Each of these is meaningful. Each of these can be guided through practical remedies. The reader gains strength when the correct category is understood, because every category has its own rhythm of correction.

Jyotisha is never a single label.

It is a complete living architecture,

---

3) The First Confirmation: The Planetary Boundary

Kaal Sarp Dosha is defined by the placement of planets within the Rahu–Ketu corridor. Therefore, the first verification is always simple and direct:

Are all the planets placed within the arc between Rahu and Ketu?

This is the foundational check.

If the planets remain inside the corridor, the formation becomes complete.

If one or more planets stand outside, the formation becomes partial or modified.

This is not a reduction of meaning. It is a refinement of meaning. In Jyotisha, refinement always strengthens interpretation. It allows the astrologer—and the reader—to see the chart as it truly is, without mixing structures.

The moment the boundary is confirmed, the horoscope becomes clearer, as if the sky itself has drawn a perfect circle around the truth.

4) The Second Confirmation: The Planet That Opens the Corridor

In some charts, one planet may stand outside the enclosure. This creates a special condition: the axis remains strong, yet the chart carries an additional stabilizing current.

That planet becomes important because it functions like a **key**.

It reveals:

- where balance naturally exists
- where strength can be built easily
- which life area becomes a stabilizing pillar
- and how remedies can be directed for faster results

In mystic terms, it is like a single lamp placed at the edge of the corridor, ensuring that the path remains illuminated.

This is why professional Jyotisha never stops at a label.

It reads the chart like a manuscript of destiny—line by line.

---

5) The Third Confirmation: Supportive Guardians in the Chart

A complete chart is never interpreted by one formation alone. The horoscope is a living system, and within that system there are always stabilizing forces that protect and strengthen the native.

Therefore, confirmation includes checking the supportive guardians:

- the strength of the **Lagna and Lagna lord**
- the stability of the **Moon**
- the guiding influence of **Jupiter**
- the discipline signature of **Saturn**
- the dignity and placement of Rahu–Ketu by sign and house

When these are strong, the formation becomes a path of focused growth and steady achievement. The native gains greater control over outcomes through disciplined routines and intelligent timing.

In mystic terms, these supportive influences are like protective circles around the seeker—ensuring that the journey remains purposeful and progressive.

---

6) The Fourth Confirmation: Timing as the Sacred Test

Jyotisha is not only about what exists.

It is about **when it speaks.**

A formation becomes most visible during certain timing windows. Therefore, confirmation also includes reading:

- the active Mahadasha and Antardasha
- periods connected to Rahu and Ketu
- transits touching the axis and sensitive points

When timing aligns, the axis becomes vivid. The native experiences sharper focus, stronger life chapters, and clear opportunities for disciplined correction.

Timing is not uncertainty.

Timing is the clock of destiny.

And the reader who understands timing gains mastery.

---

7) The Highest Confirmation: Inner Recognition

After structure and timing, there is one more confirmation that always appears—quietly, unmistakably:

the inner recognition of pattern.

The reader begins to see life as a sequence of meaningful chapters. Certain themes repeat until refined. Certain decisions carry a strong karmic weight. Certain experiences act like messages from destiny, guiding the mind toward maturity.

This recognition is not emotional.

It is luminous.

It creates a powerful state:

the seeker no longer feels confused.

The seeker feels guided.

And once guidance is felt, the remedy path becomes natural.

---

8) The Purpose of This Chapter: Clean Certainty, Strong Results

This chapter is not written to create hesitation.

It is written to create **precision.**

Because precision is power.

When Kaal Sarp Dosha is confirmed correctly:

- the mind becomes calm
- the heart becomes confident
- the reader becomes enthusiastic
- the remedies become targeted
- and results become visible through steady practice

The horoscope stops being a question.

It becomes a clear instruction.

And the reader steps forward with the most valuable gift of all:

certainty guided by wisdom.

With confirmation now established, the next chapter reveals the next level of clarity:

how the intensity of the formation is measured—so the remedies can be selected with perfect accuracy.

Chapter 5 — Severity Codes

Measuring Intensity, Mapping Strength, Selecting the Right Remedy Path

This is the chapter where the map becomes measurable.

Kaal Sarp Dosha is not approached with general statements. It is approached like an investigation: the axis is tested, its strength is measured, and its activation points are identified. When the severity level is clear, the reader gains the greatest advantage in astrology—**the ability to choose the exact remedy path that produces results.**

In Jyotisha, accurate measurement is a form of mastery. It transforms a formation from an idea into a working method. It allows the reader to move forward with clarity, because once intensity is known, remedies become focused, practical, and highly effective.

This chapter presents severity not as an emotional judgment, but as a professional code—simple to understand, powerful to apply, and designed to guide the reader toward steady improvement.

---

1) Why Severity Codes Matter

A horoscope contains many patterns, yet every pattern expresses itself with a specific intensity. Severity codes exist to answer one essential question:

How strongly is the Rahu–Ketu corridor shaping the life path right now?

When this is measured correctly, everything becomes easier:

- the reader knows what to prioritize
- the correct remedy depth becomes obvious

- progress becomes faster and more stable
- the mind gains confidence in the process

Severity measurement is not complexity. It is refinement. It is the difference between a general remedy and a perfectly aligned remedy.

2) The Three Practical Severity Codes

For applied clarity, severity can be classified into three clear codes. These codes are not labels for fear. They are levels of focus—each one indicating how concentrated the axis influence is, and how disciplined the remedy structure should be.

Code 1 — Focused Influence (Mild)

Here, the axis is present as a guiding current. The native experiences meaningful growth, clear learning cycles, and strong progress through steady discipline.

Key signatures:

- purpose-driven ambition
- strong awareness of timing
- rapid improvement through consistent routine
- visible results from simple remedies

Recommended approach:

- daily stabilization practice
- weekly spiritual discipline
- lifestyle alignment and clean habits

Code 2 — Central Influence (Moderate)

Here, the axis becomes a central theme in shaping life direction. The native benefits greatly from structured remedies, consistent practice, and decision-making refinement.

Key signatures:

- repeated life themes demanding mastery
- strong importance of planning and timing
- deeper spiritual seriousness
- strong gains through structured correction

Recommended approach:

- disciplined daily routine
- fixed weekly remedy structure
- stronger focus on mental stability practices

Code 3 — Dominant Influence (Intense)

Here, the axis becomes the primary corridor of the horoscope. The chart carries a concentrated transformation signature. With correct remedies and timing, this code produces remarkable inner strength and long-term stability.

Key signatures:

- highly focused karmic learning
- major turning points and destiny chapters
- strong need for consistency and inner control
- powerful results from sustained practice

Recommended approach:

- deep consistency in remedies

- structured long-term discipline
- strong timing-based remedy alignment

These three codes create a simple professional advantage:

the reader always knows what level of remedy structure is required.

3) The Measurement Framework: How Severity Is Tested

Severity is measured through a clear investigative framework. The following factors act like checkpoints in professional Jyotisha:

A) House Placement of Rahu and Ketu

The houses occupied by Rahu and Ketu reveal where the axis is most active. This shows the primary life chambers where learning becomes focused and progress becomes significant.

House placement answers:

- which life areas demand refinement
- where stability must be strengthened
- where transformation becomes most visible

B) Sign Strength and Dignity

The sign placement of Rahu and Ketu affects how smoothly the axis expresses itself. Certain sign conditions create a more stable flow, while others create a stronger demand for disciplined correction.

This factor answers:

- how naturally the axis energy integrates
- how quickly balance can be built through practice

C) Connection to Lagna and Moon

When Rahu–Ketu strongly influences the Lagna or Moon, the axis becomes deeply connected to personality rhythm and mental focus. This often increases the centrality of the axis and makes remedies highly responsive.

This factor answers:

- how strongly the axis shapes identity
- how strongly the axis shapes mind stability
- how quickly inner discipline produces results

D) Benefic Support and Protective Strength

Support from Jupiter, strength of the Lagna lord, and stabilizing benefic placements create a protective field around the axis influence. This increases remedy efficiency and accelerates progress.

This factor answers:

- how well the chart supports stability
- how quickly results can be established
- which remedies will work fastest

E) Planetary Contacts (Conjunctions & Aspects)

When Rahu or Ketu forms close connections with key planets, severity becomes more concentrated in that planetary domain. This helps identify the exact area where correction produces maximum improvement.

This factor answers:

- which planet is being refined through the axis
- which life theme becomes the primary training ground

4) The Role of Repetition: Destiny's Signature of Focus

One of the most reliable indicators of intensity is repetition. In Jyotisha, repetition is never accidental. It is the chart's way of highlighting the lesson that is meant to become a strength.

Repetition reveals:

- where the mind must become sharper
- where habits must become cleaner
- where choices must become more disciplined
- where progress becomes inevitable through consistency

When repetition is recognized correctly, it creates enthusiasm—because the reader sees that improvement is not random. It is structured, measurable, and achievable.

5) Severity and Remedy: The Perfect Matching Principle

This is the practical heart of the chapter:

The remedy must match the severity code.

- A focused influence responds beautifully to simple daily stabilization.
- A central influence responds powerfully to structured routines and consistent weekly discipline.
- A dominant influence responds remarkably to sustained practice and timing-based alignment.

This is why severity measurement is so valuable. It prevents waste of effort and ensures that every practice has direction. The reader gains a clear advantage:

right method → right intensity → steady results

6) Timing as the Final Confirmation

Severity becomes most visible when timing activates the axis. Dashas and transits connected to Rahu, Ketu, and the axis houses act like a spotlight that reveals the true intensity level.

When timing aligns:

- remedies produce faster stabilization
- discipline becomes easier to maintain
- progress becomes visible in real life outcomes

This is why Jyotisha is both a map and a clock.

The map shows the structure.

The clock reveals the active chapter.

---

7) The Outcome of Severity Codes: Confidence and Control

By the end of this chapter, the reader gains a clear and empowering skill:

- the ability to measure intensity
- the ability to choose the right remedy depth
- the ability to practice with confidence
- the ability to track progress steadily

This is the professional purpose of severity codes:

to turn astrology into a working system of stability and improvement.

Once severity is understood, the next step becomes natural and exciting:

to identify **the exact timing windows** when the axis becomes most active—so remedies can be applied with maximum effectiveness.

That is the focus of the next chapter.

Chapter 6 — The Trigger Window

When Destiny Turns the Key: The Hour the Axis Becomes Alive

There are moments in life that feel larger than the calendar.

The same sky is above you, the same world moves around you—

yet inside, something shifts.

The mind becomes alert.

Events begin to align with meaning.

A hidden pattern steps forward like a figure emerging from mist.

In Jyotisha, this is not coincidence.

It is **activation.**

Every horoscope contains many forces, yet each force has its own sacred hour. Kaal Sarp Dosha is a powerful formation, and its greatest gift is this: **it reveals the exact season when transformation becomes faster, deeper, and more visible.**

This chapter is the doorway where the reader learns to recognize that season. It is the chapter where astrology becomes more than interpretation—it becomes **timed mastery**.

Because when the trigger window opens, the Rahu–Ketu corridor does not merely exist in the chart.

It begins to **breathe** through life.

---

1) The Trigger Window: A Secret Hour in the Horoscope

A trigger window is the period when the Rahu–Ketu axis becomes especially active and responsive. The formation remains in the chart always, like a sacred inscription carved into destiny. Yet there are certain seasons when that inscription becomes luminous—when its meaning rises to the surface and its lessons become clearly visible.

During such windows, life gains a special vibration:

- priorities sharpen
- decisions carry deeper weight
- outcomes become more meaningful
- discipline produces quicker results
- remedies feel more powerful and alive

This is why timing is called the soul of Jyotisha.

A formation is the map.

The trigger window is the moment the map becomes a path.

---

2) The First Key: Dasha—The Royal Clock of Destiny

Dashas are not just planetary periods. They are the **royal clockwork** of the horoscope. They reveal which force is currently guiding the chapter of life.

When dashas touch Rahu and Ketu, the axis becomes vivid. The corridor begins to awaken. The seeker feels a heightened urgency to refine direction and strengthen stability.

The axis becomes strongly active during:

- **Rahu Mahadasha / Antardasha**
- **Ketu Mahadasha / Antardasha**
- dashas of planets connected closely to Rahu or Ketu

- dashas of planets placed in the axis houses
- dashas of key chart rulers when the corridor is central

During these periods, the native often experiences a rare clarity:

life is asking for maturity, and maturity is ready to rise.

In mystic terms, dasha is the hand that turns the lock.

And when it turns, destiny opens its next chamber.

---

3) The Second Key: Transits—The Moving Lights of the Sky

Transits are like moving lamps in the heavens. They travel across the chart and illuminate different areas of life. When these moving lights touch the Rahu–Ketu corridor, the axis begins to glow.

Trigger windows become strong when major transits:

- contact Rahu or Ketu directly
- activate the houses occupied by the nodes
- influence Moon or Lagna strongly
- create significant movement around the axis line

During these phases, the native experiences something extraordinary:

events begin to feel arranged, as if the universe is placing signs in sequence.

This is the secret of transits:

they do not disturb the path—

they **reveal the next step.**

---

4) The Third Key: Life Transitions—When Destiny Demands Growth

Some trigger windows arrive naturally through life transitions. These transitions are not ordinary changes. They are upgrades—moments when life invites the seeker into a higher level of responsibility and self-mastery.

Common transitions include:

- moving from study to career
- professional upgrades and new roles
- marriage, partnership, and family responsibilities
- relocation, foreign connections, new environments
- financial commitments and major investments
- leadership, public responsibility, and influence

When such transitions arrive, the axis becomes active because the native is entering a new karmic chamber. Kaal Sarp Dosha, in its highest function, acts like a guiding force—shaping the native into someone capable of holding that new life chapter with strength.

In mystic language, these moments are initiations.

Life is not testing the seeker—

life is preparing the seeker.

---

5) The Fourth Key: House Activation—Where the Corridor Speaks

The axis does not activate everywhere equally. It speaks most strongly through the houses it occupies. Each axis placement creates a unique destiny theme.

When the axis houses become activated by dasha or transit, the corridor becomes more alive. The native begins to feel a concentrated focus in that area of life:

- identity and self-mastery
- family stability and emotional grounding
- courage and action refinement
- career direction and public responsibility
- relationships and partnership evolution
- spiritual discipline and inner awakening

This is why the trigger window is not only "time."

It is also "theme."

Time opens the door.

Theme reveals the lesson waiting inside.

---

6) The Extraordinary Gift: Remedy Responsiveness

Here lies one of the most inspiring truths in Jyotisha:

When the trigger window opens, remedies become dramatically more effective.

The reason is simple: the axis is already active. The life system is already responding. The seeker's effort meets destiny's momentum.

During these windows:

- mantra practice deepens faster
- discipline becomes easier to sustain
- inner stability strengthens naturally
- clarity improves decision-making
- spiritual routines produce visible calm
- life begins to align with focused action

In other words, the trigger window is not merely a phase.

It is a season of accelerated progress.

This is why the wise do not wait passively.

They prepare actively.

And when the window opens, they step forward with confidence.

---

7) How the Seeker Uses the Window

This chapter is written to give the reader a practical advantage. When the trigger window is recognized, the seeker can use it like a sacred opportunity.

The best approach is:

- strengthen daily stability practices
- maintain consistent spiritual discipline
- refine habits and remove distractions
- focus on clear decision-making
- apply remedies with timing awareness
- build progress with steady repetition

This is where astrology becomes power.

Not because it predicts events,

but because it teaches the seeker to walk through events with mastery.

---

8) The Final Revelation: The Window Is a Doorway of Transformation

A trigger window is not simply a period.

It is a doorway.

When it opens, the seeker is invited into a higher form of life—

a life where intensity becomes focus,

focus becomes discipline,

discipline becomes stability,

and stability becomes success.

The conclusion of this chapter carries a luminous truth:

The right moment is a sacred force.

And when remedies meet the right moment, transformation becomes certain.

With this, Part I reaches completion. The reader now holds:

- the meaning of the Rahu–Ketu axis
- the formation structure of Kaal Sarp Dosha
- the method of correct confirmation
- the measurement of severity
- and the timing intelligence of trigger windows

Now the journey naturally moves forward—

into the real-life symptom file,

where the corridor's patterns are recognized clearly and refined through practical solutions.

Part II — The Symptom File

The Signs, the Patterns, and the Messages Hidden in Life Events

There is a language that destiny speaks before it becomes fully visible.

It does not always arrive as an announcement.

It arrives as a pattern.

A repeated delay.

A sudden shift.

A cycle that returns at important turning points.

An inner pressure that silently shapes decisions, emotions, and direction.

In Jyotisha, symptoms are not treated as problems. They are treated as **signals**—clear indicators that reveal where the Rahu–Ketu corridor is active and what kind of refinement is unfolding through the life path. When these signals are understood correctly, the seeker gains a powerful advantage: the ability to respond with intelligence, stability, and precise remedies.

This part of the book is designed as a professional guide to real-life patterns connected to Kaal Sarp Dosha. It follows observation, structure, and clarity. Each chapter presents a life area where the corridor may express itself, and shows how the reader can recognize the signal, strengthen the foundation, and move forward with confidence.

Because recognition is always the beginning of progress.

When the signs are read correctly, the seeker stops reacting blindly.

The seeker begins to **act wisely.**

Chapter Heads (Part II)

7. Delay Patterns

8. The Sudden Turn

9. Mind Fog

10. Restless Nights

11. Career Blocks

12. Money Leaks

13. Bond Strain

14. Health Signals

15. Spiritual Drift

Chapter 7 — Delay Patterns

When Time Itself Becomes a Teacher

Some journeys move like a straight road.

Others move like a sacred spiral—returning, refining, strengthening, and unfolding in perfect timing.

Delay patterns belong to the second kind.

In the study of Kaal Sarp Dosha, delay is not interpreted as failure. It is interpreted as **a timing signature**—a structured rhythm through which life builds maturity, strengthens decision-making, and prepares the native for stable results. The Rahu–Ketu corridor often creates a powerful relationship with time: progress happens, yet it happens with refinement, and every step becomes meaningful.

This chapter explores how delay patterns appear, why they carry purpose, and how the reader can transform waiting into steady advancement through practical methods.

Because in Jyotisha, delay is not emptiness.

Delay is **preparation.**

---

1) The Nature of Delay: A Pattern, Not a Pause

A delay pattern is not a random slowing down. It is a repeated experience where outcomes take longer than expected, even when effort is sincere. Yet within this rhythm there is always a hidden design: the native is being trained to build foundations that do not collapse.

Delay often appears as:

- results arriving after repeated attempts
- progress taking a longer route before stability forms
- success coming after refinement of skills and strategy
- opportunities opening only after inner readiness is complete

This is why delay patterns are important in Kaal Sarp Dosha study. They reveal where destiny is shaping the native into someone who can hold success with maturity.

The corridor does not deny results.

It perfects results.

---

2) Why Delay Patterns Appear in Kaal Sarp Dosha

When the Rahu–Ketu axis becomes dominant, life experiences are processed through a corridor of transformation. The native's progress becomes purposeful and structured. The axis teaches through timing, and timing teaches through refinement.

Delay patterns appear because the corridor emphasizes:

- **correct direction over quick movement**
- **stable results over temporary outcomes**
- **discipline over shortcuts**
- **skill-building over surface victory**

This is why many natives with this formation develop remarkable strength later in life. Their success becomes grounded, not fragile. Their achievements become permanent, not temporary.

In mystic terms, the corridor works like a sacred furnace:

it does not rush the gold.

It refines the gold.

3) The Most Common Forms of Delay

Delay patterns often appear in recognizable life areas. The reader may notice one or more of the following themes:

A) Delays in Career Stability

The native may progress step-by-step, gaining experience, refining capability, and eventually reaching strong positions with lasting authority.

B) Delays in Financial Comfort

Money may grow steadily through discipline and careful planning, forming a stable foundation rather than sudden rise and fall.

C) Delays in Relationships and Commitments

Partnership themes may mature slowly, leading the native toward deeper compatibility and stronger emotional intelligence.

D) Delays in Recognition

Recognition may arrive after skill mastery is complete, making the native's position respected and enduring.

In each case, delay is not denial.

It is destiny's method of building stability.

---

4) The Hidden Gift Inside Delay

Delay carries an extraordinary gift:

it strengthens the native's inner architecture.

The corridor often develops:

- patience that becomes power
- focus that becomes mastery
- resilience that becomes confidence
- discipline that becomes success
- spiritual depth that becomes clarity

The native becomes someone who does not break under pressure. Instead, pressure becomes training. And training becomes strength.

This is why delay patterns are respected in Jyotisha.

They produce maturity that cannot be purchased.

They create stability that cannot be shaken.

---

5) How to Work With Delay Patterns (Practical Strategy)

This is the most important section of the chapter: transforming the rhythm into results.

Step 1: Replace Urgency with Structure

Delay patterns respond best to organized effort. When the native works through systems—routine, planning, discipline—the corridor begins to open steadily.

Practical action:

- set weekly targets
- follow daily routines
- track progress in small measurable steps

Step 2: Strengthen the Mind's Consistency

Kaal Sarp delay patterns often reward mental stability. The mind must remain steady even when results take time.

Practical action:

- simple daily mantra discipline
- breath stabilization
- reduced distractions and clean habits

Step 3: Use Timing Intelligence

When the trigger window opens, delay patterns reduce significantly and progress becomes faster. The native benefits greatly by acting strongly during supportive periods.

Practical action:

- start major projects during favorable windows
- intensify remedies during active axis periods
- keep commitments firm and consistent

Step 4: Build Skill Before Speed

Delay patterns often disappear when skill reaches mastery level. The corridor rewards competence.

Practical action:

- learn deeply
- improve method
- refine strategy
- upgrade qualifications and practical expertise

---

6) The Spiritual Interpretation of Delay

In mystic understanding, delay is the universe creating readiness. The seeker is not being stopped. The seeker is being shaped.

Delay teaches:

- humility without weakness
- patience without passivity
- effort without exhaustion
- faith without blind dependence
- progress without instability

The corridor turns time into a teacher, and the teacher turns the seeker into a master.

---

7) The Reader's Breakthrough: Delay Becomes Direction

When the reader understands delay patterns correctly, a powerful transformation happens inside the mind:

- frustration becomes focus
- waiting becomes preparation
- repetition becomes mastery
- timing becomes strategy
- life becomes guided

The native begins to walk differently—more calmly, more intelligently, more powerfully.

Because the truth is this:

Delay is not the absence of destiny.

Delay is destiny arranging stability.

---

8) Closing Insight: The Door Opens at the Perfect Hour

Delay patterns are not permanent walls.

They are sacred gates.

And gates open when the seeker arrives with the right qualities:

- discipline
- clarity
- consistency
- and inner strength

When those qualities are built, time itself begins to cooperate. The corridor becomes a path of progress. The native rises steadily—stronger, wiser, and ready to hold success with dignity.

The journey now continues to the next chapter, where another signal is explored—

the moment life shifts suddenly, revealing the corridor's next message.

Chapter 8 — The Sudden Turn

When Life Changes Direction in One Breath

A sudden turn is the signature of a powerful chart moment—an instant when destiny rearranges the sequence of events with perfect precision. The native may not receive advance notice, yet the change arrives with remarkable timing, as though life itself has selected the exact second to redirect the journey toward a stronger outcome.

In Kaal Sarp Dosha patterns, such shifts are not interpreted as confusion. They are recognized as **high-speed alignment**—a direct expression of the Rahu–Ketu corridor, where transformation happens decisively and progress is guided through meaningful transitions. When the axis becomes active, life does not drift; it moves with purpose.

This chapter explains how sudden turns appear, what they indicate in the chart's rhythm, and how the reader can respond with calm mastery and practical intelligence—so that every change becomes an advantage and every transition becomes a step upward.

Because in Jyotisha, a sudden turn is not disorder.

It is **destiny selecting the higher route.**

---

1) What a Sudden Turn Truly Means

A sudden turn is a rapid shift that changes the direction of events. It may appear as a surprise, yet it carries a deep internal order. The native may experience:

- a sudden change in plans
- an unexpected shift in career direction

- a rapid transformation in relationships
- a new opportunity appearing without long preparation
- a swift closure of one path and opening of another

In a Rahu–Ketu dominant corridor, such shifts often function like a divine steering mechanism. The axis does not allow life to remain stagnant. It brings movement—sometimes swift, sometimes dramatic—always meaningful.

The sudden turn is not random.

It is precision in motion.

---

2) Why Sudden Turns Are Linked to the Rahu–Ketu Corridor

Rahu and Ketu represent karmic motion. Their nature is to reshape priorities and redirect growth. When their corridor becomes dominant, life becomes more sensitive to alignment.

The axis strengthens three powerful forces:

- **Rahu's acceleration** — quick movement toward new horizons
- **Ketu's detachment** – clean separation from what is complete
- **Timing intelligence** — the exact moment when the shift is most effective

This is why the sudden turn feels extraordinary. It carries a distinct vibration, as if an unseen hand has rearranged the chessboard of destiny.

In mystic terms, the corridor does not break the path.

It refines the path.

---

3) The Most Common Forms of Sudden Turns

Sudden turns often appear in specific life zones. The reader may recognize one or more of these patterns:

A) Sudden Career Redirection

A role changes, a new responsibility appears, or a new path opens unexpectedly—guiding the native toward a more meaningful direction.

B) Sudden Financial Re-Structuring

Money patterns shift quickly, leading the native to reorganize priorities and build stronger foundations.

C) Sudden Relationship Realignment

Connections evolve rapidly. The native becomes clearer about commitment, emotional truth, and deeper compatibility.

D) Sudden Inner Awakening

A shift occurs within the mind itself—new clarity, new seriousness, and a new desire to build life with purpose.

These sudden turns are not disruptions.

They are upgrades in life architecture.

---

4) The Hidden Purpose of the Sudden Turn

The sudden turn often carries one sacred message:

"The next chapter begins now."

In Kaal Sarp Dosha patterns, life teaches the seeker through decisive movement, because decisive movement produces rapid maturity.

The sudden turn often accomplishes:

- removing delays created by wrong direction
- closing distractions that waste energy
- opening opportunities aligned with growth
- strengthening courage and decision-making
- building readiness for higher responsibility

In mystic language, it is like destiny ringing a bell:

the seeker is called forward.

---

5) The Correct Response: Calm Mastery

The reader's power is not in controlling the turn.

The reader's power is in responding wisely to the turn.

A professional response includes:

Step 1: Pause and Observe

Before reacting, the seeker gathers clarity. The mind becomes quiet enough to read the message.

Step 2: Confirm the Direction

The seeker identifies what the turn is guiding toward: a new role, a new responsibility, a new discipline, a new life structure.

Step 3: Strengthen Daily Stability

The faster life moves, the more valuable daily routine becomes. Stability is created through consistent habits.

Step 4: Apply Timing-Based Remedies

During sudden shifts, remedies become highly effective because the axis is active. Discipline produces rapid stabilization.

This method transforms surprise into strategy.

And strategy transforms change into success.

6) The Mystic Signature: When Destiny Moves Faster Than Thought

The most extraordinary quality of sudden turns is how quickly they reshape reality. The native may feel that life has shifted before the mind could even prepare.

Yet the corridor always carries protection through purpose. The shift arrives because the native is ready to move forward—ready to become stronger, wiser, and more capable.

The sudden turn teaches a rare spiritual skill:

the ability to remain steady while life moves.

This steadiness becomes a lifelong advantage. It produces a mind that adapts with dignity and rises with stability.

7) Turning the Sudden Turn into an Advantage

Once the reader understands the nature of sudden turns, enthusiasm rises naturally, because the reader begins to see that life is guided.

The corridor reveals:

- why certain changes happen fast
- why certain doors close quickly
- why new doors open unexpectedly

- and how the seeker can rise immediately through disciplined action

This is the hidden power of Kaal Sarp Dosha:

it trains the native to grow in real time.

---

8) Closing Insight: The Turn Is a Sacred Signal

A sudden turn is not a loss of direction.

It is the revelation of direction.

When the Rahu–Ketu corridor activates, life may shift quickly—but it shifts with intelligence. It guides the seeker toward stability, purpose, and stronger outcomes.

When life turns suddenly, destiny is calling you forward.

Chapter 9 — Mind Fog

When Thoughts Become Mist, and Clarity Becomes a Practice

Mind fog is not silence.

It is movement without clear direction.

The mind remains active, yet the path of thought feels clouded—like walking through morning mist where shapes are present, but edges are not sharp. In Kaal Sarp Dosha patterns, this experience is deeply meaningful. It indicates that the Rahu–Ketu corridor is working on the most important instrument of destiny: **the inner compass.**

This chapter explores mind fog as a signal of refinement. It shows how the axis can intensify mental activity, how clarity can be restored through structured discipline, and how the reader can convert mental pressure into stable intelligence.

Because in Jyotisha, clarity is not a gift that arrives randomly.

Clarity is a power that is built.

---

1) What Mind Fog Really Means

Mind fog is a condition where thoughts feel many, yet conclusions feel distant. The mind moves, but the decision does not settle immediately. The native may experience:

- difficulty choosing between options
- repeated overthinking
- uncertainty even after planning
- sudden confusion in important moments
- mental tiredness despite rest

This is not weakness. It is a signal that the mind is processing a higher intensity of karmic information. The Rahu–Ketu corridor often creates a deeper mental workload, because it demands refined awareness and sharper decision-making.

Mind fog is not a limitation.

It is the mind preparing for a higher level of clarity.

---

2) Why Mind Fog Appears in Kaal Sarp Dosha

Rahu expands mental activity.

Ketu refines mental focus.

When the corridor becomes dominant, these two forces can operate together in a powerful way:

- Rahu increases the number of thoughts, possibilities, and pathways
- Ketu reduces attachment to shallow conclusions and demands deeper certainty

This combination creates a special mental signature: the mind becomes highly active, yet it refuses to settle for incomplete understanding. The native naturally seeks the "right answer," not merely a quick answer.

This is why mind fog is often connected to transformation.

It is the axis reshaping the mind into a sharper instrument.

---

3) The Most Common Forms of Mind Fog

Mind fog may appear in different patterns. Recognizing the pattern helps the reader correct it quickly.

A) Decision Fog

The native sees many options and struggles to select one confidently.

B) Memory Fog

The native remembers effort and information, yet feels a temporary dullness in recall.

C) Emotional Fog

The native senses inner pressure, yet cannot immediately define the exact emotion.

D) Direction Fog

The native feels capable, yet seeks the perfect path before taking the next step.

Each form is a message:

the mind is asking for structure.

---

4) The Hidden Gift: Mind Fog Produces Mental Mastery

In Jyotisha, every symptom carries a strength hidden inside it. Mind fog often produces extraordinary growth because it pushes the native toward:

- better thinking discipline
- stronger decision-making frameworks
- deeper spiritual seriousness
- improved focus through routine
- greater awareness of mental patterns

Over time, the native becomes someone who does not merely think—

the native learns to **command thought.**

This is one of the greatest achievements of Rahu–Ketu refinement:

the mind becomes trained, and a trained mind becomes destiny's strongest tool.

---

5) The Practical Solution Path (Clarity Protocol)

This section gives the reader a clear method to restore sharpness.

Step 1: Reduce Mental Noise

The corridor responds instantly when distractions are reduced.

Practical actions:

- limit excessive information intake
- avoid multitasking during key decisions
- keep one clear priority for the day

Step 2: Create Decision Structure

Mind fog reduces when decisions follow a simple system.

Practical actions:

- write down 3 options only
- list 3 consequences for each
- choose the one that strengthens long-term stability

Step 3: Stabilize Breath and Rhythm

The mind becomes clearer when the body becomes calm.

Practical actions:

- 7 slow breaths before important decisions
- short morning silence practice
- consistent sleep and waking time

Step 4: Use Mantra as Mental Alignment

Mantra works like a tuning key. It aligns the mind with steadiness and clarity.

Practical actions:

- a short daily mantra routine
- same time, same place
- steady repetition for stability

These steps do not require intensity.

They require consistency.

And consistency produces results.

---

6) The Axis Rule: Clarity Arrives Through Discipline

Rahu and Ketu reward discipline quickly. When the native chooses structure, the corridor begins to open. Thoughts become fewer but stronger. Decisions become slower but wiser. The mind stops scattering and begins to settle.

This is the true victory:

not the absence of thoughts,

but the presence of command.

The seeker does not fight the mind.

The seeker trains the mind.

---

7) Timing Intelligence: When Mind Fog Clears Faster

Mind fog often reduces rapidly when supportive timing is active. During favorable periods:

- decisions become easier
- inner confidence rises
- focus strengthens naturally
- remedy response becomes quicker

This is why the reader benefits from combining:

- daily discipline
- remedy consistency
- and timing awareness

When these three align, clarity becomes stable.

---

8) Closing Insight: The Mist Is a Sacred Signal

Mind fog is not the mind failing.

It is the mind refining.

It is a sacred signal that the inner compass is being upgraded. And once the upgrade completes, the native experiences something extraordinary:

clarity that does not shake,

focus that does not scatter,

and decisions that carry power.

Because the final truth is luminous:

When the Rahu–Ketu corridor refines the mind,

clarity becomes a permanent strength.

Chapter 10 — Restless Nights

When Sleep Becomes Light, and the Inner World Becomes Loud

Night is meant to be a soft sanctuary.

A sacred pause where the body rests, the mind settles, and the spirit renews itself.

Yet for some seekers, night becomes unusually alert—thoughts continue, sensations remain active, and sleep feels lighter than expected.

In the study of Kaal Sarp Dosha, restless nights are understood as a refined signal. They indicate that the Rahu–Ketu corridor is intensifying inner activity and asking the native to establish deeper mental stability. This is not a weakness of the system. It is the chart's invitation to build a stronger rhythm—where the mind learns to become calm by practice, and sleep becomes a reliable source of strength.

This chapter explores the patterns of restless nights, the reasons they appear, and the practical solutions that restore deep, steady rest.

Because in Jyotisha, sleep is not only rest.

Sleep is **recovery power.**

---

1) The Meaning of Restless Nights

Restless nights are not simply "less sleep." They are a pattern where the mind remains active during the hours meant for renewal. The native may experience:

- difficulty falling asleep quickly

- frequent waking during the night
- light sleep with repeated dreams
- mental activity continuing even in bed
- waking up tired despite time spent sleeping

In Rahu–Ketu dominant charts, this pattern often reflects an active inner corridor. The mind is processing intense impressions, reorganizing priorities, and refining its awareness. This is why the nights feel "alive."

Restless nights are not disorder.

They are inner energy seeking rhythm.

---

2) Why Restless Nights Appear in Kaal Sarp Dosha

The Rahu–Ketu axis has a natural connection with subtle mental movement.

- Rahu amplifies thoughts, impressions, and inner restlessness
- Ketu deepens inner sensitivity and spiritual alertness

When these two forces become dominant, the mind can remain active even when the body is ready to rest. The result is a night rhythm where sleep becomes lighter and the inner world becomes more vivid.

This is also why some natives experience:

- intense dream activity
- symbolic dreams
- sudden insights during night hours
- strong mental replay of day events

In mystic terms, the corridor does not allow energy to remain scattered.

It asks energy to be purified and aligned.

---

3) The Common Forms of Restless Nights

Restlessness may appear in different styles. Recognizing the type helps the reader correct it with precision.

A) Thought-Rush Nights

The mind continues planning, replaying, and thinking even after the body lies down.

B) Wake-and-Return Nights

Sleep begins, but the native wakes repeatedly and returns to sleep slowly.

C) Dream-Intensity Nights

Dreams become vivid, symbolic, or emotionally strong, creating a sense of mental activity.

D) Early-Wake Nights

The native wakes very early with alertness and finds it difficult to return to deep sleep.

Each type carries a message:

the mind is asking for stabilization.

---

4) The Hidden Gift Inside Restless Nights

Restless nights often reveal something extraordinary:

the native carries a powerful inner current.

The Rahu–Ketu corridor frequently creates individuals with:

- strong intuition
- deep sensitivity to atmosphere and energy
- sharp awareness of life patterns
- natural spiritual seriousness
- inner intelligence that works silently

When sleep is stabilized, these qualities become even stronger. The native does not lose intensity—the native gains control over intensity.

This is the true upgrade:

energy becomes disciplined, and discipline becomes peace.

---

5) The Practical Remedy Path (Night Stabilization Protocol)

This section provides simple, effective solutions that create deep rest through routine and rhythm.

Step 1: Seal the Day Before Sleep

Restless nights often reduce when the mind receives closure.

Practical actions:

- write tomorrow's top 3 tasks
- complete unfinished mental loops by listing them
- keep the final 30 minutes free of heavy thinking

Step 2: Reduce Stimulus and Light

The Rahu corridor responds strongly to reduced stimulation.

Practical actions:

- reduce screen exposure before sleep
- keep the room calm and quiet

- avoid intense conversations at night

Step 3: Breath Rhythm for Sleep

Breath is the quickest method to calm the nervous system.

Practical actions:

- slow breathing for 3–5 minutes
- gentle attention on inhale and exhale
- allow the mind to settle naturally

Step 4: Mantra as a Sleep Key

Mantra is one of the most powerful stabilizers for Rahu–Ketu activity.

Practical actions:

- repeat a chosen mantra softly
- same count daily (simple and consistent)
- keep it calm, not forceful

Mantra does not fight thoughts.

It reorganizes thought rhythm.

Step 5: Create a Sacred Sleep Routine

The corridor respects discipline. When routine is fixed, sleep becomes deeper.

Practical actions:

- fixed bedtime
- fixed waking time
- simple nightly ritual (lamp, prayer, silence)

Consistency is the secret medicine.

6) The Axis Rule: Calm Is a Skill

In Rahu–Ketu patterns, calm is not accidental.

Calm is cultivated.

The native gains peace not by suppressing the mind, but by training the mind. Over time, the night becomes stable, and sleep becomes a reliable foundation.

This produces a powerful result:

- improved clarity in the morning
- stronger emotional stability
- better decision-making
- higher productivity and confidence

When sleep becomes strong, the entire chart becomes stronger.

7) Timing Awareness: Nights Improve Faster in Supportive Periods

Restless nights often stabilize rapidly when timing becomes supportive. During favorable phases:

- the mind settles more easily
- dreams become calmer
- sleep becomes deeper
- remedies work faster

This is why the reader benefits from a steady routine, especially during axis-active periods. Timing becomes a wind of support, and practice becomes more effective.

8) Closing Insight: The Night Can Become a Sanctuary Again

Restless nights are not permanent.

They are a signal of inner energy seeking alignment.

When the seeker applies steady discipline, sleep becomes deeper, the mind becomes calmer, and the body recovers fully. The night returns to its true purpose: renewal, strength, and inner restoration.

The final truth of this chapter is luminous:

When the Rahu–Ketu corridor is stabilized,

night becomes sacred again—

and the seeker awakens with power.

Chapter 11 — Career Blocks

When Progress Demands Precision, and Work Becomes a Path of Mastery

A career is not only a profession.

It is a field where destiny reveals competence, timing, and inner strength.

In certain life phases, effort rises like a steady flame—yet the outer results appear slower than expected. The seeker continues working, learning, improving, and building, but the path feels guarded by invisible gates. In Jyotisha, this is not interpreted as denial. It is interpreted as **refinement**—a sacred process through which the horoscope shapes a stronger foundation before granting stable expansion.

In Kaal Sarp Dosha patterns, career blocks often appear as signals from the Rahu–Ketu corridor. They indicate that the native is being trained for **higher-level stability**, where success is not temporary, but enduring. The corridor does not reduce progress. It sharpens progress. It turns work into mastery, and mastery into authority.

This chapter explores career blocks as meaningful patterns, explains their logic through the axis, and offers practical methods to transform resistance into reliable rise.

Because in Jyotisha, career is not only income.

Career is **dharma in action.**

---

1) What Career Blocks Really Indicate

Career blocks are moments where movement feels restricted even when effort is sincere. The native may experience:

- slow promotions despite capability
- repeated delays in recognition
- sudden interruptions in professional flow
- obstacles before a breakthrough
- unstable job phases followed by rebuilding

In Kaal Sarp Dosha, these patterns are not random. They often appear when the Rahu–Ketu corridor is shaping the native's professional identity. The chart is refining competence, strengthening decision-making, and preparing the native for long-term stability.

The block is not the end.

The block is the shaping point.

---

2) Why the Rahu–Ketu Corridor Affects Career Flow

Career is strongly connected to karma. It reflects the native's responsibilities, skills, timing, and public role. Rahu and Ketu influence career in a unique way:

- **Rahu** pushes ambition upward and intensifies the desire for achievement
- **Ketu** refines ego and demands deeper mastery before expansion

When both operate strongly, the career path becomes purposeful. The native is guided away from superficial progress and toward structured growth. The corridor encourages the seeker to become not only successful, but capable of holding success with dignity.

In mystic terms, the axis does not block the crown.

It strengthens the head that will wear it.

3) The Common Career Block Patterns

Career blocks often appear in specific forms. Recognizing the form reveals the remedy direction.

A) The "Effort Without Visibility" Pattern

Work is strong, results are real, yet recognition comes later. This pattern builds skill and authority quietly before public acknowledgment.

B) The "Near Success" Pattern

Opportunities come close, then delay slightly. This pattern refines preparation and timing so the final success becomes stable.

C) The "Sudden Shift" Pattern

The role changes unexpectedly. The native is guided into a new path that ultimately fits better and produces stronger growth.

D) The "Rebuilding Phase" Pattern

The career resets or restructures. This pattern builds long-term stability by removing weak foundations and strengthening the core.

Each pattern is a message:

success is being shaped into permanence.

4) The Hidden Gift: Career Blocks Create Mastery

Career blocks often produce extraordinary inner strength. They build qualities that become lifelong assets:

- discipline under pressure
- patience with purpose
- strategy over impulse
- humility with ambition
- skill-based confidence

This is why many natives with Kaal Sarp Dosha develop remarkable careers over time. Their success becomes deep-rooted. Their authority becomes respected. Their growth becomes lasting.

The corridor trains the native not for quick rise,

but for **unshakable rise.**

---

5) The Practical Strategy: Turning Blocks into Breakthroughs

This section gives a direct professional method.

Step 1: Convert Effort into Measurable Skill

The corridor rewards competence. Skill becomes the strongest remedy in career matters.

Practical actions:

- upgrade qualifications
- strengthen communication and execution
- master one high-value expertise
- build a visible portfolio of results

Step 2: Build a Career Routine (Not Just a Job Routine)

A job gives income. A career gives direction. The corridor responds to long-term planning.

Practical actions:

- set 6-month goals
- track weekly progress
- create one clear specialization
- maintain consistent professional discipline

Step 3: Align with Timing

When the trigger window opens, the corridor becomes highly responsive. This is the best time for:

- job changes
- promotions and negotiations
- new ventures
- leadership roles

Timing awareness turns effort into advantage.

Step 4: Strengthen Authority Through Stability

Authority is not demanded. It is built.

Practical actions:

- show reliability
- maintain consistency
- avoid emotional reactions in professional spaces
- protect reputation through calm speech and strong results

The corridor always supports those who build stability.

---

6) Mystic Career Remedy: Work as a Sacred Discipline

In Jyotisha, karma is refined through action. When career becomes disciplined, it becomes a remedy itself. The seeker begins to work with a deeper awareness:

- work becomes practice
- practice becomes mastery
- mastery becomes recognition
- recognition becomes stable success

This is one of the most powerful secrets of Kaal Sarp Dosha:

the remedy is not only ritual—

the remedy is also refined action.

When action becomes sacred, destiny cooperates faster.

7) Signs of Approaching Breakthrough

Career blocks often dissolve when the native reaches a specific level of readiness. Signs that the breakthrough phase is near include:

- clearer opportunities appearing
- stronger confidence in decision-making
- improved stability in daily routine
- recognition beginning to increase
- supportive timing activating career houses

This phase often feels extraordinary:

as if the invisible gate has opened quietly,

and progress begins to flow.

8) Closing Insight: The Corridor Builds the Crown Slowly

A career block is not a rejection.

It is refinement before expansion.

The Rahu–Ketu corridor shapes the native into someone who can hold success without losing balance. It turns ambition into skill, skill into authority, and authority into stability.

The conclusion of this chapter is luminous:

When career progress is refined through discipline,

success becomes permanent—

and the seeker rises with dignity and power.

Chapter 12 — Money Leaks

When Wealth Slips Quietly, and Prosperity Demands Protection

Money is energy in motion.

It arrives through effort, skill, timing, and responsibility.

Yet sometimes, even when income is present, prosperity feels unusually delicate—as if wealth enters the hand, but slips through invisible cracks before it becomes stable.

In Jyotisha, this is not seen as misfortune. It is read as a **signal of refinement**. In Kaal Sarp Dosha patterns, money leaks often appear as a message from the Rahu–Ketu corridor: *strengthen the financial foundation, purify the flow, and protect the energy of earning.*

This chapter explores money leaks as a practical symptom, explains their deeper logic, and offers structured solutions that convert financial drift into lasting stability.

Because in Jyotisha, prosperity is not only earning.

Prosperity is **retaining with wisdom.**

---

1) What Money Leaks Really Mean

Money leaks are not always large losses. Often, they appear as small, repeated drains that reduce long-term stability. The native may experience:

- expenses increasing without clear reason
- savings failing to grow despite income
- repeated small financial obligations
- sudden repair costs and unplanned spending

- lending money that returns slowly
- spending driven by emotional pressure

In Kaal Sarp Dosha charts, these patterns often reflect a corridor lesson: wealth must be managed with structure, not impulse. The axis is teaching the native to handle money as a disciplined force.

The leak is not weakness.

The leak is a call for financial mastery.

---

2) Why the Rahu–Ketu Corridor Influences Money Flow

Rahu expands desire and urgency.

Ketu refines attachment and removes unnecessary excess.

When these two operate strongly, the native's financial life may show a distinct rhythm:

- income may come through strong effort and ambition
- expenses may increase through scattered priorities
- financial stability improves greatly through discipline and simplicity

The corridor does not oppose wealth.

It demands **clean wealth**—wealth that is stable, protected, and aligned with long-term growth.

In mystic terms, Rahu brings the river.

Ketu shapes the riverbank.

Without the riverbank, water flows away.

---

3) The Most Common Types of Money Leaks

Money leaks often appear in recognizable forms:

A) The "Invisible Expense" Leak

Small, frequent spending that seems harmless but becomes heavy over time.

B) The "Emergency Drain" Leak

Unexpected repairs, medical costs, travel expenses, or urgent obligations appearing repeatedly.

C) The "Helping Hand" Leak

Money given to others repeatedly, sometimes without clear boundaries, creating financial imbalance.

D) The "Comfort Spending" Leak

Spending driven by stress relief, emotional pressure, or the desire to feel immediate ease.

E) The "Scattered Investment" Leak

Multiple financial moves without a single clear strategy, reducing long-term stability.

Each type is a message from the corridor:

prosperity needs structure to become permanent.

---

4) The Hidden Gift: Money Leaks Build Financial Wisdom

Money leaks often create one extraordinary strength:

the native becomes financially intelligent.

Over time, the corridor trains the seeker to develop:

- stronger budgeting discipline
- better planning and savings habits
- clearer priorities
- improved risk management
- mature financial decision-making

This is why many natives with Kaal Sarp Dosha eventually become excellent at wealth management. They learn through patterns, refine through experience, and rise with stable prosperity.

The corridor does not remove wealth.

It teaches wealth to stay.

---

5) The Practical Solution Path (Wealth Protection Protocol)

This is where the reader gains direct control.

Step 1: Seal the Leaks First

Before increasing income, stop unnecessary outflow.

Practical actions:

- track spending for 14 days
- identify the top 3 drains
- reduce one drain immediately
- create a fixed monthly limit

Step 2: Build a Simple Savings Structure

The corridor rewards steady, consistent saving more than irregular saving.

Practical actions:

- automatic savings transfer
- separate savings account
- fixed percentage saving rule
- emergency fund as priority

Step 3: Strengthen Boundaries

Money leaks often reduce when boundaries become clear.

Practical actions:

- avoid unplanned lending
- delay major purchases by 48 hours
- use a "need vs. desire" filter

Step 4: Create One Financial Focus

The axis supports focus. Scattered financial goals reduce stability.

Practical actions:

- one primary investment plan
- one long-term goal
- one skill upgrade for income growth

Focus becomes protection.

---

6) Mystic Financial Remedy: Wealth as a Sacred Responsibility

In Jyotisha, wealth is not merely currency.

It is Lakshmi-tattva—prosperity energy.

When wealth is treated with respect, it responds with stability. The corridor teaches the seeker to handle money with awareness:

- earn with discipline
- spend with intelligence
- save with devotion
- invest with clarity

This creates a powerful shift:

money stops feeling unstable,

and begins to feel guided.

---

7) Timing and Money Flow

Money leaks often reduce significantly during supportive timing periods. When favorable dashas and transits activate financial houses, the corridor becomes more cooperative.

During such phases:

- income stabilizes
- expenses become manageable
- savings growth becomes smoother
- remedies show faster results

This is why timing awareness is a financial advantage. The reader learns when to expand and when to consolidate.

---

8) Closing Insight: Prosperity Stays Where Respect Lives

Money leaks are not permanent.

They are refinement signals.

When the seeker applies structure, discipline, and stable habits, prosperity begins to hold. The corridor becomes a guide, teaching the native to build wealth that remains steady through time.

The conclusion of this chapter is luminous:

When wealth is protected with wisdom,

Lakshmi stays—

and prosperity becomes a lasting companion.

Chapter 13 — Bond Strain

When Relationships Demand Depth, and Connection Becomes Sacred Refinement

A bond is not only a relationship.

It is a living thread of energy—woven through trust, communication, timing, and emotional truth.

Sometimes, even when love and sincerity exist, the connection feels unusually sensitive. Words carry extra weight. Silence feels louder. Small misunderstandings appear like ripples that must be calmed with care. In Jyotisha, this is not interpreted as weakness in relationships. It is interpreted as a sign of **deep refinement**—a signal that the horoscope is shaping the native into a person capable of stronger emotional mastery and more stable connection.

In Kaal Sarp Dosha patterns, bond strain often appears when the Rahu–Ketu corridor is training the native to upgrade relationship intelligence. The corridor does not reduce connection. It purifies connection. It removes confusion and builds clarity, so that relationships become stable, meaningful, and spiritually aligned.

This chapter explores bond strain as a signal, explains why it appears, and offers practical methods to restore harmony and deepen emotional stability.

Because in Jyotisha, relationships are not only companionship.

Relationships are **karmic mirrors of growth**.

---

1) What Bond Strain Really Means

Bond strain is a pattern where relationships feel pressured even when intentions are good. The native may experience:

- emotional distance appearing suddenly
- misunderstandings increasing without clear reason
- difficulty expressing feelings smoothly
- repeated sensitivity in communication
- feeling misunderstood despite sincerity
- a sense of emotional imbalance in giving and receiving

In Kaal Sarp Dosha, such patterns often indicate that the axis is active in relationship chambers. The corridor is strengthening emotional discipline and communication maturity.

Bond strain is not a break.

Bond strain is a refinement phase.

---

2) Why the Rahu–Ketu Corridor Affects Relationships

Relationships are deeply connected to mind and karma. Rahu and Ketu influence relationships through two powerful movements:

- **Rahu intensifies desire, expectations, and emotional urgency**
- **Ketu refines attachment, reduces illusion, and demands truth**

When the corridor becomes strong, relationships become more meaningful. They cannot remain casual or superficial. The axis invites depth, sincerity, and stable emotional conduct.

In mystic terms, the corridor acts like a sacred fire:

it removes smoke from the bond,

so the flame becomes pure.

3) The Most Common Forms of Bond Strain

Bond strain often appears in recognizable styles:

A) The "Misunderstood Words" Pattern

Communication becomes sensitive. Even simple statements may feel heavier than intended.

B) The "Distance and Return" Pattern

Closeness and silence alternate. The bond moves in waves, asking for stability.

C) The "Expectation Pressure" Pattern

One side may feel more responsibility or emotional demand. Balance must be restored through clarity.

D) The "Trust Refinement" Pattern

The relationship seeks stronger honesty and transparency, strengthening the foundation.

Each form carries a message:

the bond is becoming deeper and more mature.

4) The Hidden Gift: Bond Strain Builds Emotional Mastery

Bond strain often creates an extraordinary inner strength:

the native becomes emotionally intelligent.

The corridor trains the seeker to develop:

- patience in communication
- clarity in expression
- calmness under emotional pressure
- ability to listen deeply
- capacity to hold relationships with maturity

This is why relationships connected to Kaal Sarp Dosha often become very strong over time. The bond becomes stable because it is refined, not rushed.

The corridor does not reduce love.

It teaches love to become wise.

---

5) The Practical Solution Path (Harmony Protocol)

This is where the reader gains control and confidence.

Step 1: Replace Reaction with Response

The corridor rewards calm speech and controlled emotion.

Practical actions:

- pause before replying
- speak slowly during sensitive discussions
- avoid immediate conclusions

Step 2: Clarify Expectations

Many bond strains reduce when expectations are expressed cleanly.

Practical actions:

- discuss responsibilities gently
- define boundaries with respect

- create mutual clarity in commitments

Step 3: Strengthen Trust Through Consistency

Trust grows through repeated reliability, not occasional intensity.

Practical actions:

- keep promises
- maintain emotional steadiness
- avoid sudden withdrawal

Step 4: Create a Weekly Bond Ritual

Small consistent bonding practices stabilize relationships powerfully.

Practical actions:

- weekly calm conversation time
- shared prayer or silence
- simple acts of support and appreciation

Consistency becomes the healing force.

---

6) Mystic Relationship Remedy: Sacred Speech and Inner Cleanliness

In Jyotisha, words are energy.

Speech can bless a bond or burden it.

The Rahu–Ketu corridor responds strongly to **clean speech**:

- truthful
- gentle
- stable

- and purposeful

When speech becomes sacred, relationships become calmer. The bond becomes protected.

In mystic terms, the remedy is simple:

purify the voice,

and the bond becomes luminous.

---

7) Timing and Relationship Stability

Bond strain often increases during active axis periods and reduces significantly during supportive timing. When the timing is favorable:

- communication becomes easier
- emotional clarity improves
- harmony strengthens naturally
- remedies show faster results

This is why timing awareness is a relationship advantage. The seeker learns when to speak deeply, when to stay calm, and when to strengthen routine harmony practices.

---

8) Closing Insight: The Bond Becomes Stronger Through Refinement

Bond strain is not a sign of failure.

It is a sign of depth.

When the seeker applies calm discipline, respectful communication, and stable routines, the relationship becomes stronger than before. The corridor refines the bond into something mature, stable, and spiritually aligned.

The conclusion of this chapter is luminous:

When love is guided by wisdom,

relationships become unbreakable—

and harmony becomes destiny's gift.

Chapter 14 — Health Signals

When the Body Speaks in Symbols, and Wellness Becomes a Sacred Discipline

The body is not separate from destiny.

It is destiny's most faithful messenger.

Long before the mind understands a lesson, the body often gives a signal—softly at first, then more clearly—guiding the seeker toward better rhythm, stronger discipline, and deeper self-care. In Jyotisha, these signals are not viewed with worry. They are viewed with respect, because the body is a sacred instrument through which the soul completes its life path.

In Kaal Sarp Dosha patterns, health signals often appear as **refinement markers**. They indicate that the Rahu–Ketu corridor is asking the native to stabilize routine, purify habits, and strengthen the nervous system through consistent practice. When the seeker responds correctly, the result is powerful: energy becomes steady, clarity improves, and wellness becomes a lasting foundation.

This chapter explores health signals in a practical and positive way, showing how the corridor guides the reader toward stronger vitality and long-term balance.

Because in Jyotisha, health is not only survival.

Health is **spiritual strength in the body.**

---

1) What Health Signals Mean in Kaal Sarp Dosha

Health signals are not always major conditions. Often, they appear as repeated minor patterns that indicate the body is asking for better alignment. The native may notice:

- energy fluctuations
- fatigue after mental stress
- digestive sensitivity
- sleep rhythm changes
- tension-related discomfort
- irregular appetite or routine imbalance

These are not signs of weakness. They are signs of sensitivity. The Rahu–Ketu corridor often creates a heightened inner intensity, and the body responds by requesting discipline and rhythm.

The signal is not fear.

The signal is guidance.

2) Why the Rahu–Ketu Corridor Influences the Body

Rahu and Ketu influence the body through the nervous system, habit rhythm, and mental pressure.

- **Rahu** can intensify pace, stimulation, and mental activity
- **Ketu** can refine the body's need for simplicity, purity, and steady routine

When these forces become dominant, the body becomes more sensitive to:

- irregular sleep
- irregular meals
- emotional stress

- excessive stimulation
- inconsistent routines

This is why the corridor often trains the seeker to become disciplined. Once discipline is established, the body becomes stronger, calmer, and more stable.

In mystic terms, the corridor is not demanding perfection.

It is demanding **alignment**.

---

3) The Common Health Signal Patterns

Health signals often appear in recognizable forms:

A) Energy Rise and Drop Pattern

The native feels strong for some hours, then suddenly feels drained. This improves greatly with stable routine.

B) Stress Sensitivity Pattern

The body reacts quickly to mental pressure. Calm practices and rhythm create strong balance.

C) Sleep Rhythm Pattern

Rest becomes lighter or irregular. Night stabilization practices restore deep recovery.

D) Digestive Rhythm Pattern

The body becomes sensitive to irregular eating and rushed meals. Simplicity restores strength.

E) Tension Accumulation Pattern

Neck, shoulders, head, or general body tension increases when the mind is overloaded. Breath discipline helps greatly.

Each pattern is a message:

the body wants rhythm.

---

4) The Hidden Gift: Health Signals Create Self-Mastery

One of the most extraordinary benefits of Kaal Sarp Dosha refinement is that it can make the seeker deeply aware of the body. This awareness becomes a powerful advantage.

Over time, the native develops:

- better self-control
- cleaner lifestyle discipline
- improved energy management
- stronger emotional stability
- long-term wellness intelligence

The corridor teaches the seeker to become their own healer through routine and awareness.

This is not limitation.

This is mastery training.

---

5) The Practical Solution Path (Vitality Stabilization Protocol)

This section gives a simple and highly effective wellness structure.

Step 1: Fix Daily Rhythm

The body becomes strong when rhythm becomes stable.

Practical actions:

- fixed sleep and waking time
- fixed meal timings
- consistent morning routine

Step 2: Reduce Over-Stimulation

Rahu patterns respond quickly when stimulation is reduced.

Practical actions:

- limit excessive screen time
- avoid late-night heavy mental work
- reduce overthinking through simple planning

Step 3: Strengthen Breath Discipline

Breath is the fastest stabilizer of the nervous system.

Practical actions:

- slow breathing for 3–5 minutes daily
- gentle morning breathing practice
- calm breathing before sleep

Step 4: Build Simple Movement

The corridor supports steady movement more than intense irregular exercise.

Practical actions:

- daily walking
- light stretching
- consistent body activation

Step 5: Use Spiritual Routine as Wellness

In Jyotisha, spiritual discipline supports physical balance.

Practical actions:

- daily prayer or mantra
- lamp lighting routine
- short silence practice

Consistency becomes protection.

---

6) Mystic Wellness Remedy: The Body as a Temple

In the deeper tradition, the body is treated as a temple.

A temple is kept clean, calm, and disciplined—not for fear, but for sacred strength.

When the seeker treats health as sacred:

- food becomes respectful
- sleep becomes disciplined
- speech becomes calmer
- habits become cleaner
- energy becomes stable

This creates a powerful shift: the body becomes a strong vessel for destiny.

---

7) Timing and Health Stability

Health signals often become more noticeable during axis-active periods and improve greatly during supportive timing. When timing is favorable:

- energy stabilizes

- sleep improves
- digestion becomes calmer
- remedies work faster

This is why timing awareness is a wellness advantage. The reader learns when to strengthen routine and when to focus on recovery practices.

---

8) Closing Insight: The Body Speaks to Protect the Path

Health signals are not warnings.

They are guardians.

They guide the seeker toward better discipline and stronger vitality. When the reader responds with steady routine and calm practice, wellness becomes a stable foundation, and life becomes smoother, clearer, and more powerful.

The conclusion of this chapter is luminous:

When the body is honored with discipline,

health becomes strength—

and destiny becomes easier to carry.

Chapter 15 — Spiritual Drift

When the Inner Flame Weakens, and the Soul Calls for Reconnection

Spirituality is not always lost in loud ways.

Sometimes it fades quietly—like a lamp whose flame remains, yet grows smaller when the wind changes.

The seeker continues life, responsibilities continue, time moves forward, yet the inner connection feels lighter than before. Prayer becomes irregular. Silence becomes rare. The heart feels less drawn toward sacred routine, even though the soul still respects it deeply.

In Jyotisha, this is not interpreted as decline. It is interpreted as a **recalibration signal**—a message from the Rahu–Ketu corridor that the inner rhythm must be restored, because spiritual discipline is not only devotion. It is stability, protection, and inner power.

In Kaal Sarp Dosha patterns, spiritual drift often appears when the axis is refining the seeker's relationship with faith, practice, and inner direction. The corridor is guiding the native toward a deeper, more consistent connection—one that does not depend on mood, but on mastery.

This chapter explores spiritual drift with clarity and warmth, showing how it appears, why it happens, and how the seeker can return to a stronger inner alignment through simple, practical methods.

Because in Jyotisha, spirituality is not escape.

Spirituality is **the root of strength.**

---

1) What Spiritual Drift Really Means

Spiritual drift is a phase where the inner connection becomes less consistent. The seeker may experience:

- loss of interest in daily prayer routines
- reduced mantra discipline
- less desire for temple visits or spiritual reading
- feeling "too busy" for inner practice
- spiritual enthusiasm rising and falling in waves
- difficulty maintaining silence or meditation

This is not a negative sign. It is a natural cycle in a life that is evolving. The corridor often creates intense worldly focus at certain phases, and the inner world asks to be rebalanced gently.

Spiritual drift is not disconnection.

It is a call for renewal.

---

2) Why the Rahu–Ketu Corridor Creates Spiritual Drift

Rahu pulls energy toward the outer world—goals, achievement, urgency, responsibility.

Ketu pulls energy toward inner truth—meaning, refinement, silence, spiritual maturity.

When both operate strongly, the seeker may temporarily lean toward one side. During strong Rahu phases, the mind becomes highly engaged with worldly progress. Spiritual routine may become lighter, not because devotion is absent, but because attention is concentrated elsewhere.

Then Ketu begins to speak again—quietly, insistently—calling the seeker back toward inner alignment.

This is why spiritual drift is meaningful:

it shows the axis is active in shaping balance.

In mystic terms, the corridor does not remove devotion.

It upgrades devotion into discipline.

---

3) The Common Forms of Spiritual Drift

Spiritual drift often appears in recognizable patterns:

A) The "Routine Break" Pattern

A consistent spiritual routine becomes irregular due to work, travel, or responsibilities.

B) The "Dry Devotion" Pattern

Prayer continues, but the emotional sweetness feels reduced. The seeker needs renewal.

C) The "Mind Noise" Pattern

The mind remains active and distracted, making silence feel difficult.

D) The "Faith Distance" Pattern

The seeker feels spiritual respect, yet does not feel emotionally connected in the same way.

Each pattern carries one message:

the inner flame wants steady oxygen.

---

4) The Hidden Gift: Drift Creates Deeper Spiritual Strength

Spiritual drift often leads to a stronger return. It teaches the seeker an extraordinary truth:

faith becomes powerful when it becomes consistent.

The corridor trains the seeker to build:

- devotion without dependency
- practice without emotional fluctuation
- spirituality as a daily foundation
- calmness as a disciplined skill
- inner strength that remains steady in all phases

This is the spiritual maturity Kaal Sarp Dosha often produces:

a seeker who becomes stable from within.

---

5) The Practical Solution Path (Reconnection Protocol)

This section gives simple methods that create powerful spiritual return.

Step 1: Begin Small, Never Heavy

The corridor responds to consistency more than intensity.

Practical actions:

- 3 minutes daily prayer
- one mantra repetition cycle
- one short silence practice

Small practice done daily becomes a strong spiritual shield.

Step 2: Fix One Sacred Time

A fixed time builds spiritual stability.

Practical actions:

- morning after bath

- evening before sleep
- same place, same rhythm

Time becomes a temple.

Step 3: Create a Simple Lamp Routine

Light is a powerful symbol for Rahu–Ketu refinement.

Practical actions:

- light a lamp daily
- offer one silent prayer
- keep the mind calm and focused

This restores sacred atmosphere inside the home and inside the mind.

Step 4: Spiritual Reading as Mind Purification

The corridor responds beautifully to sacred knowledge.

Practical actions:

- read one page daily
- listen to one short spiritual discourse
- maintain steady learning

Knowledge becomes nourishment.

Step 5: Weekly Deepening

Daily practice stabilizes. Weekly deepening strengthens.

Practical actions:

- temple visit
- longer prayer session

- charity or seva
- silence practice

This keeps the flame bright.

---

6) Mystic Remedy: Devotion as Inner Protection

In Jyotisha, devotion is not only worship.

It is protection.

When spiritual practice becomes consistent:

- the mind becomes calmer
- fear reduces naturally
- decision-making improves
- emotional stability strengthens
- destiny becomes easier to carry

This is why spiritual drift is important to correct gently. It restores the seeker's inner shield.

In mystic terms, devotion creates a circle of light around the path.

---

7) Timing and Spiritual Return

Spiritual drift often appears during strong Rahu activity and reduces when Ketu periods or supportive transits encourage inner focus. During such phases:

- interest in mantra returns naturally
- silence becomes easier
- devotion becomes sweeter
- remedies feel more alive

Timing becomes an invisible support. The seeker simply needs to maintain the practice so the timing can amplify it.

8) Closing Insight: The Flame Returns When Routine Becomes Sacred

Spiritual drift is not permanent.

It is a phase of recalibration.

When the seeker restores daily practice—even in small form—the inner flame grows steady again. The corridor becomes aligned, the mind becomes calm, and devotion becomes strong.

The conclusion of this chapter is luminous:

When the seeker returns to spiritual rhythm,

the soul becomes powerful again—

and destiny becomes illuminated from within.

Part III — The Remedy Vault

The Secret Method of Kaal Sarp Mastery: Simple, Hidden, Unbreakable

This is the part of the book where everything becomes real.

Not as theory.

Not as belief.

Not as imagination.

As method.

Because Kaal Sarp Dosha is not solved by discussion.

It is stabilized by practice—a practice so precise, so consistent, and so intelligently designed that the Rahu–Ketu corridor begins to respond like a disciplined force.

There is a secret known to serious practitioners of Jyotisha:

the Rahu–Ketu axis does not require countless rituals.

It requires one thing above all:

a single powerful system performed without break.

This is the hidden key.

When the seeker performs a correct system daily—without drama, without delay, without confusion—something extraordinary begins to happen. The mind becomes quieter, not by struggle, but by alignment. The inner pressure becomes organized. The life path becomes protected. Decisions become clean. The atmosphere around the seeker changes, as if an invisible circle has formed—subtle, steady, unmistakable.

This is not poetic exaggeration.

This is the nature of the nodes.

Rahu and Ketu respond to rhythm.

They respond to repetition.

They respond to sacred discipline.

That is why this section is called The Remedy Vault. It is not a collection of random solutions. It is a carefully locked sequence—built like a spiritual mechanism. Each chapter opens one door. Each door reveals a method. Each method strengthens the seeker until stability becomes natural and progress becomes steady.

Here, remedies are not presented as superstition.

They are presented as spiritual technology—practical actions designed to stabilize the mind, protect timing, strengthen prosperity, and restore inner command.

And at the center of this vault is the most exceptional truth of all:

Kaal Sarp Dosha becomes powerless in the presence of disciplined mastery.

Not because the chart changes—

but because the seeker changes.

This part is written for those who want results that can be felt in real life:

clearer mornings, calmer nights, stronger decisions, stable progress, and a steady inner confidence that does not shake.

The seeker does not need complicated rituals.

The seeker needs a method that can be practiced anywhere, by anyone, every day.

That method begins here.

Chapter Heads (Part III)

16. The Hidden Key

17. The Daily Shield

18. The Mantra Method

19. The Lamp Discipline

20. The Water Purification

21. The Charity Key

22. The Temple Circuit

23. The Home Protection Grid

24. The 30-Day Reset

25. The Final Seal

Chapter 16 — The Hidden Key

The One Secret Method That Makes Every Remedy Work Faster

This chapter is not an explanation.

It is an initiation into method.

Because there is a difference between knowing remedies and **activating remedies**. Many seekers perform practices with sincerity, yet they do not experience full results—not because the remedies are weak, but because the remedies are not arranged into a single living system.

Kaal Sarp Dosha responds to one principle above all others:

Rahu–Ketu responds to rhythm.

Not occasional action.

Not scattered effort.

Not random intensity.

Rhythm.

When a seeker builds a fixed rhythm, the corridor begins to reorganize itself. The mind becomes calm, timing becomes smoother, and the invisible pressure of life becomes manageable. This is the hidden key that experienced practitioners recognize immediately:

one system, performed daily, without break, becomes a shield.

This chapter gives that system—simple enough to practice anywhere, powerful enough to change the inner atmosphere of life.

---

1) The Secret of the Nodes: Why Rhythm Controls the Axis

Rahu and Ketu are not ordinary forces. They do not respond best to emotion. They respond best to **pattern.**

A single disciplined pattern—repeated daily—creates an inner structure that the axis cannot disturb. This is why the Rahu–Ketu corridor becomes stable when routine becomes stable.

In practical terms:

- when the day begins with order, the mind stays ordered
- when the mind stays ordered, decisions become clean
- when decisions become clean, life becomes smoother
- when life becomes smoother, the corridor becomes protective

This is the first law of Kaal Sarp mastery:

discipline is not effort—it is architecture.

---

2) The Hidden Key Method (The 12-Minute Axis Lock)

This is the exceptional method.

It is short. It is repeatable. It is powerful.

And it works because it is designed to align directly with the Rahu–Ketu corridor.

The Rule

Do this **daily**, preferably at the **same time**, for **40 days** without break.

If time is limited, do the minimum version.

If time is available, do the full version.

Step A — Water Seal (1 minute)

Take a small amount of clean water in your right palm.

Close your eyes for a moment.

Mentally affirm:

"My mind is calm. My path is protected. My destiny is stable."

Sip the water slowly.

This is not superstition.

It is a signal to the nervous system: the day begins with control.

Step B — Breath Lock (2 minutes)

Sit comfortably. Keep spine straight.

Do slow breathing:

- inhale gently
- exhale longer than inhale
- repeat calmly for 2 minutes

Breath is the fastest stabilizer of Rahu influence.

It reduces scattered thinking and creates inner authority.

Step C — Mantra Bandhana (6 minutes)

Choose **one mantra** and keep it fixed.

Recommended universal mantra for stability:

Om Namah Shivaya

Repeat it slowly, with attention, for 6 minutes.

No speed. No force. Only rhythm.

The power is not in volume.

The power is in steadiness.

This step is the axis lock.

It binds the mind to a single vibration.

Step D — Light Command (2 minutes)

Look at a lamp flame (or a candle flame).

If a lamp is not available, imagine a steady flame at the center of the forehead.

Mentally affirm:

"Light leads me. Wisdom protects me. I act with clarity."

This is the spiritual reset of perception.

It weakens mental fog and strengthens direction.

Step E — One-Line Seal (1 minute)

End with a single sentence spoken aloud:

"Today I walk in discipline, and discipline protects me."

This is the final seal.

It converts spirituality into action.

---

3) Why This Method Works (The Logic of Power)

This method works because it completes a full circuit:

- **Water** stabilizes the inner element and beginning energy
- **Breath** stabilizes the nervous system and thought rhythm
- **Mantra** stabilizes the mind and karmic corridor
- **Light** stabilizes perception and direction
- **Sankalpa** stabilizes action and outcome

It is not many remedies.

It is one system.

And one system is what Rahu–Ketu obeys.

---

4) The Three Signs the Hidden Key Has Activated

Within days, the seeker begins to notice:

1. **A calmer morning mind**
2. **Better decision clarity**
3. **Reduced inner pressure and restlessness**

These are not imagination.

These are alignment signals.

When the axis is aligned, the mind stops scattering.

And when the mind stops scattering, destiny becomes easier to carry.

---

5) The Mistakes That Reduce Remedy Power

This method is strong, but it must be protected from dilution. Avoid:

- changing mantra frequently
- practicing only when mood is good
- doing remedies randomly without timing
- skipping days and restarting repeatedly

The corridor responds to consistency.

Not intensity.

---

6) The Professional Rule: Keep It Simple, Keep It Sacred

The reader must remember this:

A small practice done daily is stronger than a big practice done rarely.

This is the hidden key that separates real results from temporary enthusiasm.

---

7) When to Practice for Maximum Results

Best times:

- early morning
- after bath
- before beginning work
- or at sunset if mornings are not possible

Most important rule:

same time daily creates maximum axis stability.

---

8) Closing Seal: The One Practice That Opens All Doors

This chapter gives the reader the master-key.

Once this is established, every other remedy becomes faster, smoother, and more powerful.

Because this method does not fight the axis.

It trains the axis.

And the final truth is exceptional:

When the seeker becomes rhythmic,

the Rahu–Ketu corridor becomes protective.

Chapter 17 — The Daily Shield

The Protection Routine That Makes the Day Obey Your Discipline

A shield is not something you hold only in danger.

A true shield is something you wear before the world touches you.

In the Rahu–Ketu corridor, the day itself becomes a field of energies—thoughts, people, timing, pressure, opportunity, responsibility. The seeker does not need to fear any of these. The seeker needs one thing:

a daily protection rhythm.

This chapter gives the *Daily Shield*—a practical routine that creates a stable inner boundary, strengthens mental command, and keeps the life-path protected from unnecessary disturbance. It is designed to work with real life schedules. It is simple enough to practice daily, yet powerful enough to change the atmosphere around the seeker.

Because when the shield is active, the mind stays calm, the tongue stays controlled, the actions stay correct—and destiny begins to cooperate.

---

1) What the Daily Shield Really Is

The Daily Shield is not a long ritual.

It is a **sequence of protection actions** performed with consistency.

It works because Rahu–Ketu does not respond to scattered effort. It responds to structured repetition. The shield is built from three layers:

1. **Inner shield** (mind stability)
2. **Outer shield** (speech and action discipline)

3. **Timing shield** (right decisions at the right moment)

When these three layers combine, the seeker experiences a powerful change:

life becomes smoother, and progress becomes steady.

---

2) The Daily Shield Routine (Morning Method — 7 Minutes)

This is the protection method for daily use.

It is short, repeatable, and highly effective.

Step 1 — The First Silence (1 minute)

Sit quietly. Eyes half closed.

Do not chase thoughts. Do not fight thoughts.

Simply sit.

This creates the first protection circle:

the mind stops rushing into the day.

Step 2 — The Breath Barrier (2 minutes)

Breathe slowly and deeply.

- inhale gently
- exhale longer than inhale
- repeat calmly

This builds the nervous system shield.

It reduces mental scattering and strengthens inner control.

Step 3 — The Mantra Shield (3 minutes)

Repeat your fixed mantra:

Om Namah Shivaya

Do it softly, steadily, and with rhythm.

This is the protective vibration layer.

It creates a stable frequency around the mind.

Step 4 — The Command Seal (1 minute)

Speak one line aloud:

"Today my mind is steady, my speech is pure, my path is protected."

This is not only prayer.

This is programming the day with discipline.

---

3) The Work-Day Shield (Micro Practices That Protect You Outside)

Kaal Sarp Dosha is not managed only in prayer time.

It is managed in real life moments—when decisions are made.

Use these micro shields during the day:

A) The 3-Breath Rule

Before any major reply, decision, or signature:

take 3 slow breaths.

This stops impulsive action and strengthens timing intelligence.

B) The One-Sentence Rule

In sensitive conversations:

speak one sentence, then pause.

This protects relationships, reputation, and clarity.

C) The Delay-to-Strength Rule

If confused:

delay the decision for 30 minutes and return with calm mind.

This protects against Rahu-style urgency and strengthens precision.

These are shields that work invisibly—yet powerfully.

---

4) The Evening Shield (Closing the Day Without Carrying Weight)

Many seekers lose energy not during the day, but after the day—when the mind carries unfinished impressions into the night.

The Evening Shield prevents this.

Step 1 — One Gratitude Line

Speak one sentence:

"I am grateful for today's learning and protection."

Step 2 — One Release Line

Speak one sentence:

"I release all unnecessary weight from my mind."

Step 3 — One Mantra Cycle

Repeat **Om Namah Shivaya** for 1–3 minutes.

This closes the day cleanly.

A clean closure creates deep sleep and fresh mornings.

5) The Shield Rules (Strict, Simple, Powerful)

To keep the Daily Shield effective, follow these rules:

- keep the same mantra daily
- practice at the same time as much as possible
- never increase complexity unnecessarily
- consistency is more important than duration
- calmness is more important than speed

This creates the most powerful result:

the shield becomes automatic.

6) Signs the Daily Shield Is Working

Within days of consistency, the seeker may notice:

- reduced emotional reaction
- better clarity before speaking
- improved sleep quality
- stronger confidence in decisions
- smoother interactions with people
- steady progress without mental pressure

These are the signs of protection becoming active.

7) The Mystic Truth: Protection Is a Vibration

In Jyotisha, protection is not only physical.

Protection is a vibration.

When the seeker holds the right vibration:

- the mind becomes calm
- the speech becomes clean
- the actions become correct
- and timing becomes friendly

This is why the Daily Shield is so powerful.

It changes the seeker's field.

And when the field changes, the path changes.

---

8) Closing Seal: The Day Becomes Your Ally

The Daily Shield is not a ritual for fear.

It is a method for mastery.

Once it becomes consistent, the seeker begins to experience something extraordinary:

the day feels less heavy, less noisy, less uncertain.

The mind remains stable.

The path becomes protected.

Because the final truth is clear:

When the seeker begins the day with discipline,

destiny walks with protection.

Chapter 18 — The Mantra Method

The Sacred Code of Sound That Stabilizes the Rahu–Ketu Corridor

A mantra is not merely a word.

It is a command made of vibration.

It enters the mind like a key enters a lock—quietly, precisely, and without force. And when the key is correct, something extraordinary happens: the inner world becomes organized. Thought becomes disciplined. Emotion becomes steady. The seeker begins to move through life with a protected rhythm, as if an unseen order has formed around the path.

This is why mantra is the crown-method in Kaal Sarp Dosha remedies.

Because the Rahu–Ketu corridor does not respond fastest to logic alone.

It responds fastest to **frequency**.

This chapter presents the Mantra Method in a professional, practical, and deeply powerful way—so the reader can practice it with confidence and experience real results through consistency.

Because in Jyotisha, mantra is not superstition.

Mantra is **spiritual technology**.

---

1) Why Mantra Works on Kaal Sarp Dosha

Kaal Sarp Dosha is an axis formation.

Axis formations influence the mind first, and life events next.

The mind is the command center of destiny.

When the mind is stable, the corridor becomes stable.

Mantra works because it creates three direct effects:

1. **It reduces mental scattering** (Rahu calmness)
2. **It strengthens inner detachment from fear and confusion** (Ketu clarity)
3. **It builds a steady rhythm that the axis obeys** (corridor control)

This is the secret:

Rahu and Ketu respond to rhythm more than emotion.

---

2) The First Rule of Mantra Power: One Mantra Only

The greatest mistake seekers make is changing mantras frequently.

In Kaal Sarp Dosha remedies, mantra works best when it becomes a single fixed vibration in the life of the practitioner.

One mantra. One rhythm. One path.

This creates an inner signature that becomes stronger each day.

It becomes a living protection.

The rule is absolute:

⟐ Choose one mantra

⟐ Stay with it

⟐ Repeat daily

⟐ Do not switch without reason

This is how mantra becomes power.

---

3) The Mantra Method Structure (The Three-Layer System)

A complete mantra method has three layers.

This is the professional structure used by disciplined practitioners.

Layer 1 — The Daily Mantra (Foundation)

This is the mantra repeated every day, without break.

Recommended universal foundation mantra:

Om Namah Shivaya

It is stable, pure, and deeply protective.

Layer 2 — The Focus Mantra (Strengthening)

This is repeated when the seeker wants extra stability during active axis windows, important decisions, or intense life phases.

A strong strengthening mantra:

Om Sham Shanicharaya Namah *(for discipline and stability)*

or

Om Dum Durgayai Namah *(for protection and inner courage)*

This is not to replace the daily mantra.

This is to strengthen the system when needed.

Layer 3 — The Silence Seal (Completion)

After mantra, the seeker sits in silence for a short time.

Even **30 seconds** is enough.

Silence is the final seal that locks the mantra vibration inside the mind.

---

4) Correct Count: The Secret of Measurable Results

Mantra gives the best results when it has count discipline.

Count discipline creates rhythm.

Rhythm creates axis control.

Use these practical levels:

Level A — Minimum Daily Count

27 repetitions

This is the smallest complete cycle for daily continuity.

Level B — Strong Daily Count

54 repetitions

This builds stability quickly.

Level C — Master Daily Count

108 repetitions

This is the classic discipline count for deep results.

The reader may choose any one level and keep it fixed daily.

The power is not in choosing the highest count.

The power is in choosing the count that will never be broken.

---

5) Correct Timing: When Mantra Becomes Unstoppable

Mantra becomes most powerful when practiced at a consistent time.

Best timing options:

- early morning
- after bath
- before work begins
- sunset time
- before sleep

The best rule is simple:

Same time daily = maximum results.

The Rahu–Ketu corridor respects timing discipline.

When timing becomes fixed, the mantra becomes a living shield.

6) Correct Seat and Direction (Simple, Effective Rules)

This is not about complexity.

It is about sacred order.

Practical rules:

- sit in one fixed place daily
- face east or north if possible
- keep the spine straight
- keep the mind calm
- avoid rushing the mantra

Even if none of these are possible, the mantra still works.

But when these are followed, the vibration becomes stronger.

7) The Voice Rule: How to Chant Correctly

Mantra can be repeated in three modes:

1. **Loud voice** (for energy and focus)
2. **Soft voice** (best for daily practice)
3. **Mental repetition** (best in public or silent environments)

For Kaal Sarp Dosha, the best daily method is:

soft voice or mental repetition with full attention.

Because attention is the true fuel of mantra.

---

8) The Protection Rule: What to Do When the Mind Wanders

The mind will wander.

That is natural.

The power is not in forcing the mind.

The power is in returning it.

When distraction happens:

- pause for one breath
- return to the mantra
- continue without irritation

This creates the real mastery:

the seeker becomes stronger than the mind's restlessness.

---

9) The Mantra Completion Seal (The One-Line Finish)

At the end of chanting, speak one sentence:

"This vibration protects my mind and strengthens my destiny."

This sentence seals the practice into daily life.

It transforms mantra from prayer into command.

---

10) The 40-Day Rule: The Axis Must Obey Continuity

The Rahu–Ketu corridor responds dramatically to a 40-day uninterrupted cycle.

40 days is the activation key.

If the reader completes 40 days without break:

- the mind becomes steadier
- sleep improves
- clarity increases
- decision-making strengthens
- inner fear reduces naturally
- life becomes smoother

This is why the 40-day discipline is treated as a sacred contract.

---

11) Closing Insight: Mantra Is the Highest Remedy

Many remedies support Kaal Sarp Dosha.

But mantra is the central remedy because it reaches the root: the mind.

And when the mind becomes stable, everything becomes stable.

The final truth of this chapter is luminous:

When one mantra becomes your daily rhythm,

the Rahu–Ketu corridor becomes your protector.

Chapter 19 — The Lamp Discipline

The Flame That Commands Shadows and Makes the Path Luminous

Some remedies work through action.

Some work through discipline.

And some work through a presence so subtle, so ancient, and so powerful—

that the mind begins to settle the moment it is performed.

The lamp is one such remedy.

A flame is not merely light.

It is a symbol of mastery. It is the visible form of inner clarity. It stands against darkness without struggle—silent, steady, undefeated. This is why the lamp discipline is one of the most respected practices for Rahu–Ketu stabilization.

Kaal Sarp Dosha is an axis of shadow and transformation. And the most direct answer to shadow is not argument, not fear, not complexity. The answer is **steady light**.

This chapter reveals a method that feels extraordinary in its simplicity. It is practical enough for daily life, yet carries a mystic aura that the seeker can feel immediately. When practiced with consistency, the lamp becomes a shield, a purifier, and a silent force that strengthens the entire destiny rhythm.

Because in Jyotisha, light is not decoration.

Light is **command.**

1) Why the Lamp Works on the Rahu–Ketu Corridor

Rahu represents shadow movement, illusion, restlessness, and urgency.

Ketu represents subtle withdrawal, karmic refinement, and spiritual intensity.

A lamp flame has three direct effects on this corridor:

1. **It stabilizes perception** — the mind becomes calmer and clearer
2. **It purifies the atmosphere** — the space becomes spiritually lighter
3. **It creates a daily sacred rhythm** — rhythm is what the nodes obey

This is why lamp discipline is powerful.

It does not fight the axis.

It reorganizes the axis.

---

2) The Golden Rule: The Flame Must Be Steady

The lamp discipline is not about how big the flame is.

It is about how steady the flame is.

A steady flame trains the mind to become steady.

And when the mind becomes steady, the corridor becomes cooperative.

This is the hidden truth:

The flame outside becomes the flame inside.

---

3) The Lamp Discipline Method (Daily Practice — 5 Minutes)

This is the exact method designed for daily use.

It is simple, repeatable, and exceptionally effective.

Step 1 — Prepare the Space (30 seconds)

Choose a clean, quiet place in your home.

Keep it fixed daily if possible.

Even a small corner becomes sacred when used consistently.

Step 2 — Light the Lamp (30 seconds)

Light a lamp using oil or ghee.

If a traditional lamp is not available, a candle is acceptable.

The method is not dependent on luxury.

It is dependent on sincerity and rhythm.

Step 3 — The Silent Flame Gaze (2 minutes)

Sit comfortably.

Look gently at the flame without staring harshly.

Allow the mind to settle into the flame's steadiness.

This step is extremely powerful because it stabilizes:

- scattered thoughts
- inner restlessness
- emotional pressure
- mental fog

The flame becomes a silent teacher.

Step 4 — The Light Mantra (2 minutes)

Repeat softly:

Om Namah Shivaya

Or repeat:

Om Deepa Jyothi Parabrahma *(traditional lamp invocation)*

Keep the repetition calm and slow.

The power is in rhythm.

Step 5 — The Seal Line (30 seconds)

Speak one line:

"This light protects my mind and purifies my destiny."

Then bow the head slightly.

This seals the practice into the day's energy.

---

4) The Weekly Strengthening (One Day Extra Power)

Once per week, add one strengthening layer.

On that day:

- keep the lamp burning a little longer (10–15 minutes if possible)
- maintain silence near the flame
- offer a simple prayer for stability and clarity

This weekly extension strengthens the protective field of the home and the mind.

The corridor responds strongly to weekly rhythm.

---

5) What the Lamp Discipline Corrects (Direct Benefits)

With consistent practice, the seeker experiences:

- calmer mornings
- smoother decision-making
- reduced mental noise
- better sleep quality
- improved emotional stability
- increased confidence and inner control
- stronger spiritual presence in the home

These results appear because the lamp creates a stable vibration that the axis respects.

Light does not argue with darkness.

Light simply remains.

---

6) The Mistakes That Reduce Lamp Power

To keep the practice exceptionally effective, avoid:

- lighting the lamp only occasionally
- doing it with haste and distraction
- changing time daily without reason
- treating it like decoration instead of discipline

The lamp is a remedy when it becomes a routine.

---

7) Best Time for Lamp Discipline

The best times are:

- **sunrise** (for mental clarity and daily protection)
- **sunset** (for removing heaviness and stabilizing the evening)
- **before sleep** (for calmness and dream purification)

Choose one time and keep it fixed.

This makes the method unstoppable.

---

8) The Mystic Secret: The Lamp Is a Boundary of Light

In the subtle tradition, the lamp is not only light.

It is a boundary.

A daily lamp creates a quiet spiritual wall around the seeker's path. It strengthens the home atmosphere, reduces unwanted mental disturbances, and builds a protected rhythm that feels almost tangible.

This is why the practice feels extraordinary:

it changes the field.

When the field changes, the path changes.

---

9) Closing Insight: The Flame Becomes a Guardian

The lamp discipline is one of the simplest remedies in the world—

and one of the strongest.

Because it carries a truth that the Rahu–Ketu corridor cannot resist:

steady light creates steady destiny.

When the seeker lights the lamp daily, the mind becomes luminous, the home becomes calm, and the life path becomes protected.

The final seal of this chapter is luminous:

When the flame is lit with discipline,

shadows retreat—

and the seeker walks forward in clarity.

Chapter 20 — The Water Purification

The Cleansing Method That Resets the Inner Current and Seals Protection

Water remembers.

Not as a theory—

as a sacred truth recognized by every ancient tradition that mastered energy, mind, and discipline. Water carries vibration, absorbs atmosphere, and restores balance with silent authority. That is why, in remedies for Kaal Sarp Dosha, water is not treated as a simple element. It is treated as a purifier, a stabilizer, and a carrier of command.

The Rahu–Ketu corridor is a corridor of intensity. It can accelerate thoughts, increase inner pressure, and make the mind feel unusually active. Water purification is the remedy that cools the corridor, clears the inner field, and restores calm rhythm—so the seeker moves through life with steadiness.

This chapter gives a method that is exceptionally practical, yet mystically powerful. It can be practiced anywhere. It requires no complexity. And when done with consistency, it becomes one of the strongest stabilizers in the entire Remedy Vault.

Because in Jyotisha, purification is not an idea.

Purification is **power in action.**

---

1) Why Water Purification Works on Kaal Sarp Dosha

The Rahu–Ketu axis influences subtle rhythm—mind rhythm, sleep rhythm, emotional rhythm, decision rhythm. When rhythm becomes unstable, the seeker needs a remedy that restores smoothness without force.

Water purification works because it creates three direct effects:

1. **Cooling effect** — reduces inner heat and restlessness
2. **Cleansing effect** — clears subtle heaviness and mental fog
3. **Reset effect** — refreshes the day's energy and restores clarity

This is why water is used in sacred disciplines:

it stabilizes without struggle.

---

2) The Golden Rule: Purification Must Be Gentle

This method is not aggressive.

It is calm, steady, and disciplined.

Rahu–Ketu responds to:

- gentleness
- repetition
- rhythm

The more calm the method, the more powerful the result.

Because the corridor is corrected by stability, not by force.

---

3) The Water Purification Method (Daily Practice — 4 Minutes)

This is the daily method.

It is simple, repeatable, and exceptionally effective.

Step 1 — Prepare the Water (30 seconds)

Take a clean glass or copper vessel with fresh water.

Hold it in your right hand.

Step 2 — The Silent Charge (30 seconds)

Close your eyes.

Do not rush.

Allow the mind to become quiet.

This is the moment the water receives your command.

Step 3 — The Purification Mantra (2 minutes)

Repeat softly while holding the water:

Om Namah Shivaya

Keep the repetition slow and steady.

This creates a purified vibration in the water and inside the mind simultaneously.

Step 4 — The Sip Seal (30 seconds)

Sip the water slowly in **three small sips.**

Each sip is a sealing act.

As you sip, mentally affirm:

- **Sip 1:** "My mind is calm."
- **Sip 2:** "My path is protected."
- **Sip 3:** "My destiny is stable."

Step 5 — The Final Touch (30 seconds)

Sprinkle a few drops of water on the crown of the head.

This is a traditional completion gesture.

It seals the purification as a full reset.

---

4) The Weekly Power Version (Stronger Cleansing Day)

Once per week, add the enhanced method.

On that day:

- prepare water
- repeat the mantra for 5 minutes
- sip slowly
- and wash the face gently with the same water

This produces a deeper purification effect and strengthens inner stability.

The corridor responds strongly to weekly reinforcement.

---

5) What Water Purification Corrects (Practical Results)

With consistent practice, the seeker may experience:

- reduced inner restlessness
- improved emotional balance
- calmer thought rhythm
- smoother decision-making
- better sleep and dream calmness
- increased sense of protection
- clearer morning energy

These results occur because water stabilizes the inner field quietly, without pressure.

It cleanses the unseen weight that the mind carries.

---

6) The Mistakes to Avoid

To keep this method exceptionally strong, avoid:

- doing it in a hurry
- practicing with distracted mind
- skipping days repeatedly
- changing the mantra frequently
- treating it as a casual act

The method becomes powerful when it becomes sacred routine.

---

7) Best Timing for Water Purification

The best times are:

- early morning (for clean daily start)
- before leaving home (for protection)
- after returning home (for cleansing outer influence)
- before sleep (for calming the mind)

Choose one timing and keep it steady.

Timing discipline increases power.

---

8) Mystic Secret: Water Purification Seals the Aura

In the subtle tradition, water purification is also aura discipline. It refreshes the seeker's field and removes invisible heaviness.

When performed daily, the seeker feels:

- lighter
- calmer
- clearer
- more protected
- more stable

This is why the method feels extraordinary.

It works not only on the body, but on the atmosphere around the body.

---

9) Closing Insight: Purification Creates Authority

Kaal Sarp Dosha responds to inner authority.

Water purification creates that authority quietly.

It cools the mind.

It strengthens clarity.

It seals protection.

The final truth of this chapter is luminous:

When water is purified with mantra,

the seeker becomes purified with stability—

and destiny becomes smooth.

Chapter 21 — The Charity Key

The Secret Exchange That Converts Karma into Protection

Some remedies work through mantra.

Some work through discipline.

But one remedy works through a law so ancient, so exact, and so powerful—

that even unseen destiny begins to soften and cooperate.

That law is **charity.**

In Jyotisha, charity is not simply kindness.

It is a sacred exchange mechanism. It moves energy, purifies karmic weight, and creates protection that cannot be manufactured by effort alone. When performed correctly, charity becomes a direct key for Rahu–Ketu stabilization—because the nodes respond strongly to the act of giving with discipline.

Kaal Sarp Dosha is a corridor of transformation. And transformation becomes smooth when the seeker learns one secret:

what is released with purity returns as protection.

This chapter reveals the Charity Key as a practical method—clear, structured, repeatable—so the reader can practice it confidently and experience its power in real life.

Because in Jyotisha, charity is not loss.

Charity is **destiny correction.**

1) Why Charity Works on the Rahu–Ketu Axis

Rahu and Ketu influence karma directly. They refine desire, attachment, and life direction. Charity becomes powerful because it produces three direct effects:

1. **It purifies urgency** (Rahu becomes calmer)
2. **It strengthens detachment** (Ketu becomes clearer)
3. **It activates protection** (the corridor becomes cooperative)

Charity creates an inner signature that says:

"I am not controlled by fear. I am guided by dharma."

And dharma is always protected.

---

2) The Charity Key Rule: Give Small, Give Pure, Give Consistently

The power of charity is not in the size.

The power is in the purity and repetition.

Kaal Sarp remedies become unstoppable when charity is:

- simple
- consistent
- respectful
- and done with sincerity

The nodes respond to rhythm.

Charity is rhythm in action.

---

3) The Charity Key Method (Weekly Practice — 10 Minutes)

This is the exact method for real-life use.

It is practical, powerful, and easy to maintain.

Step 1 — Fix One Charity Day

Choose one day every week and keep it fixed.

Examples:

- Monday
- Thursday
- Saturday

Any day is acceptable.

The power comes from **fixed repetition.**

Step 2 — Choose One Charity Item

Keep it simple. Choose only one category:

- food (most powerful and immediate)
- clothes (practical and stabilizing)
- medicine support (highly protective)
- educational help (very auspicious)
- temple donation (clean and sacred)

Do not change categories every week.

One consistent channel becomes stronger.

Step 3 — Give With a Silent Mantra

Before giving, repeat mentally:

Om Namah Shivaya

Just 9 repetitions are enough.

This charges the charity with sacred intention.

Step 4 — Give Without Announcement

Give quietly.

Do not seek attention.

Do not speak about it widely.

This is important because the nodes respond to purity, not publicity.

Step 5 — Seal the Charity

After giving, speak one line softly:

"May this act protect my mind and purify my destiny."

This seals the karma exchange.

---

4) The Three Highest-Power Charity Forms

For Kaal Sarp Dosha stabilization, these are exceptionally effective:

A) Feeding

Giving food to someone in need, or supporting a meal distribution.

This directly purifies Rahu urgency and builds protection.

B) Supporting the Vulnerable

Helping elderly, differently-abled persons, or those in recovery.

This activates deep karmic blessings.

C) Supporting Education

Helping students with books, fees, or learning support.

This strengthens destiny clarity and long-term stability.

These are not random categories.

They are karma-correcting channels.

5) The Charity Shield: What It Corrects

With consistent weekly charity, the seeker begins to notice:

- smoother life flow
- reduced unexpected disturbances
- calmer mind under pressure
- improved luck in timing-based events
- better emotional stability
- stronger sense of protection
- progress becoming steady and guided

This happens because charity releases karmic pressure.

And when pressure reduces, destiny becomes lighter.

6) The Mistakes That Reduce Charity Power

To keep the method exceptional, avoid:

- giving only when troubled
- giving irregularly and forgetting
- giving with impatience or irritation
- giving while expecting immediate return
- changing charity forms repeatedly

The axis responds to consistency and purity.

Charity is strongest when it becomes a vow-like rhythm.

7) The Charity Timing Secret (When to Give for Maximum Power)

The most effective times:

- morning hours
- before food (simple discipline)
- after prayer
- on fixed weekly day

But the highest rule is:

same day, same method, repeated weekly.

This builds a karmic protection wall around the life path.

---

8) Mystic Truth: Charity Creates an Invisible Guardian

In the subtle tradition, charity creates a protective presence.

It is not visible, but it is real.

The seeker begins to feel:

- less heaviness
- less fear
- more calm confidence
- better clarity
- and smoother movement in life chapters

This is the Charity Key at work.

It does not change the world outside immediately—

it changes the field around the seeker.

And when the field changes, destiny changes.

---

9) Closing Seal: The Secret Exchange Is Always Successful

Charity is not a random act.

It is a spiritual law.

When performed with discipline, it becomes one of the most powerful remedies for Kaal Sarp Dosha. It purifies the corridor, strengthens the mind, and creates protection that follows the seeker silently.

The final truth of this chapter is luminous:

When you give with purity,

karma becomes lighter—

and destiny becomes brighter.

Chapter 22 — The Temple Circuit

The Sacred Route That Reorders Destiny and Activates Protection

A temple is not only a place.

It is a living field.

When you enter a temple, you do not enter a building—you enter a vibration that has been strengthened by centuries of prayer, mantra, discipline, and divine presence. The air itself carries stability. The silence itself carries protection. Even the footsteps feel different, as though the ground remembers devotion.

This is why temple worship is one of the most powerful remedies for Kaal Sarp Dosha.

The Rahu–Ketu corridor is subtle. It shapes timing, thought, and inner pressure. And the most direct way to stabilize subtle forces is to enter a space where stability is already established. A temple is that space. It is a spiritual circuit breaker that resets the mind, purifies the field, and restores inner command.

This chapter gives a precise method called **The Temple Circuit**—a step-by-step practice that any seeker can perform. It is simple enough to be real, yet powerful enough to feel extraordinary. When practiced consistently, it becomes a living shield around the destiny path.

Because in Jyotisha, temple worship is not tradition alone.

Temple worship is **alignment technology**.

---

1) Why the Temple Circuit Works on Kaal Sarp Dosha

Kaal Sarp Dosha is an axis formation.

Axis formations respond best to **field correction.**

The temple provides exactly that. It creates:

1. **Mind correction** — calmness becomes immediate
2. **Aura correction** — heaviness reduces naturally
3. **Timing correction** — decisions become cleaner and smoother
4. **Protection activation** — the path feels guarded and guided

The temple circuit works because it places the seeker inside a stronger vibration than the mind's restlessness.

In mystic truth:

the temple does not change your destiny—

it changes your destiny's atmosphere.

---

2) The Golden Rule: Go With One Intention Only

Many seekers enter a temple with many thoughts.

This reduces the power.

For Kaal Sarp Dosha remedies, the temple becomes strongest when the intention is singular:

"I seek stability, clarity, and protection."

One intention creates one direction.

One direction creates one result.

---

3) The Temple Circuit Method (Step-by-Step)

(Weekly Practice — 20 Minutes, Extremely Powerful)

This is the exact method.

Follow it as written. Keep it consistent.

Step 1 — Prepare Before Leaving Home (2 minutes)

Before stepping out, stand quietly.

Repeat mentally **9 times**:

Om Namah Shivaya

Then speak one line:

"I walk into sacred space, and I return with protection."

This is the opening seal.

Step 2 — Enter the Temple in Silence (1 minute)

Do not speak while entering.

Let the mind become quiet.

The first minute inside a temple is a sacred doorway.

Treat it as a threshold.

Step 3 — Offer the First Prayer (2 minutes)

Stand before the main deity.

Hands joined. Eyes calm.

Offer a simple prayer:

"May my mind become steady.

May my path become clear.

May my destiny become protected."

This is enough.

Simplicity is power.

Step 4 — The Clockwise Circuit (Pradakshina) (5 minutes)

Walk slowly around the sanctum **clockwise.**

Do **3 rounds** if possible.

If time is limited, do **1 round.**

While walking, repeat mentally:

Om Namah Shivaya

This is the true circuit.

It reorganizes the inner rhythm.

The corridor responds to movement with mantra.

Step 5 — The Offering (3 minutes)

Offer any one simple item:

- flowers
- a small oil lamp
- a coconut
- a small donation
- prasadam support

The offering is not a transaction.

It is an alignment act.

It says:

"I release ego, and I receive grace."

Step 6 — The Stillness Seat (5 minutes)

Sit quietly inside the temple compound.

No phone. No talking. No restlessness.

Just sit.

This stillness is one of the most powerful remedies for Rahu–Ketu.

Because silence is the opposite of mental scattering.

Even 3 minutes is strong.

5 minutes is exceptional.

Step 7 — The Exit Seal (2 minutes)

Before leaving, look once again at the deity.

Bow the head gently and speak inwardly:

"The protection remains with me."

Then exit without hurry.

This completes the circuit.

---

4) The Best Temples for Rahu–Ketu Stabilization

Any sincere temple works.

But these are especially powerful in corridor refinement:

- Shiva temples

- Devi temples
- Subrahmanya temples
- temples with strong daily lamp worship

Choose one temple and keep it fixed weekly if possible.

Repetition creates a stronger spiritual bond.

---

5) The Temple Circuit Rules (Strict and Powerful)

To keep this remedy exceptional, follow these rules:

- go on the same day weekly
- keep the same temple when possible
- enter in silence
- do at least one pradakshina
- do not rush the visit
- keep the mind calm and focused

These rules convert temple worship into a method, not an event.

---

6) What the Temple Circuit Corrects

With consistent practice, the seeker may notice:

- reduced inner pressure
- increased mental clarity
- smoother progress in plans
- improved emotional stability
- better sleep rhythm
- stronger confidence in decisions
- a sense of spiritual protection around the life path

This happens because the temple strengthens the seeker's field.

---

7) The Mystic Secret: The Temple Creates a Destiny Shield

The most extraordinary truth is this:

A temple is not only a place you visit.

It becomes a force that follows you.

When the seeker visits consistently, the temple's vibration begins to remain within the seeker's atmosphere. The home becomes calmer. The mind becomes steadier. The path becomes protected.

This is not imagination.

This is spiritual physics.

---

8) Closing Insight: The Circuit Becomes a Sacred Armor

The Temple Circuit is one of the most powerful remedies in this entire vault because it requires no complexity—only sincerity and repetition.

And repetition is what Rahu–Ketu obeys.

The final truth of this chapter is luminous:

When the seeker walks the sacred circuit,

destiny becomes lighter—

and protection becomes permanent.

Chapter 23 — The Home Protection Grid

Turning Your Home into a Shield of Light, Calm, and Destiny Stability

A home is not only walls and rooms.

A home is a field.

It holds the echoes of thought, the residue of emotion, the vibration of words spoken inside it, and the invisible atmosphere created by daily life. When the Rahu–Ketu corridor is active, the home must become more than a resting place. It must become a **stabilization zone**—a space where the mind becomes quiet, sleep becomes deep, and destiny becomes protected.

This is why the Home Protection Grid is one of the most exceptional methods in this Remedy Vault.

It is not complicated.

It is not expensive.

It is not dramatic.

But it is powerful—because it works through the most important law of Kaal Sarp mastery:

what is repeated daily becomes unbreakable.

This chapter gives a step-by-step system that the reader can practice immediately. It builds a sacred grid inside the home—simple enough for anyone, strong enough to feel extraordinary, and practical enough to maintain without struggle.

Because in Jyotisha, protection is not only outside.

Protection begins **where you live.**

---

1) Why the Home Must Be Protected in Kaal Sarp Dosha

The Rahu–Ketu corridor influences:

- thought rhythm
- sleep rhythm
- emotional rhythm
- timing rhythm

If the home atmosphere is restless, the corridor becomes stronger.

If the home atmosphere is calm, the corridor becomes cooperative.

The Home Protection Grid works because it creates:

- a stable mental environment
- a purified spiritual atmosphere
- a rhythm of daily discipline
- a protective boundary around the seeker

The home becomes a temple of stability.

---

2) The Golden Rule: The Grid Must Be Simple and Permanent

Many people try complicated rituals and stop.

That weakens results.

This method is designed to be permanent.

The rule is:

Small daily actions, fixed in place and time, create the strongest protection.

The nodes obey rhythm.

The grid is rhythm made visible.

---

3) The Home Protection Grid (Daily System — 10 Minutes Total)

This is the complete method.

It is divided into three zones:

1. **Entrance Zone** (outer energy filter)
2. **Prayer Zone** (inner stability center)
3. **Sleep Zone** (night protection seal)

Follow these steps as a fixed daily system.

A) The Entrance Zone (2 Minutes)

The First Gate of Protection

The entrance is where energy enters.

So the first protection must begin there.

Step 1 — Keep the Entrance Clean

A clean entrance is a clean signal to destiny.

Practical rule:

- remove clutter
- keep the doorway simple and clear

This alone strengthens the home's stability.

Step 2 — Water Drop Seal

Keep a small bowl or cup of clean water near the entrance (inside the home).

Every evening, replace it with fresh water.

This acts as a subtle absorber of heaviness.

Step 3 — One-Line Command

Before entering fully, say softly:

"Only peace and clarity enter this home."

This sentence is a boundary of vibration.

B) The Prayer Zone (5 Minutes)

The Central Generator of Light

Choose one fixed corner in the home.

This becomes the stability point.

You do not need a large altar.

You need a fixed place.

Step 1 — Light the Lamp (1 minute)

Light a lamp daily.

A steady flame creates a steady field.

Step 2 — Mantra Rhythm (3 minutes)

Repeat:

Om Namah Shivaya

Slowly, calmly, with attention.

This becomes the home's protective vibration.

Step 3 — Silent Seal (1 minute)

Sit silently and feel the calm.

This locks the grid into the atmosphere.

The home begins to feel different—lighter, calmer, protected.

C) The Sleep Zone (3 Minutes)

The Night Seal That Protects Mind and Dreams

Night is when Rahu–Ketu becomes more active in subtle ways.

So the sleep zone must be protected.

Step 1 — No Noise Rule

Reduce unnecessary talk and heavy discussions at night.

The corridor becomes calm when the night becomes calm.

Step 2 — Bedside Mantra Seal

Before sleep, repeat mentally:

Om Namah Shivaya *(27 times)*

This creates a calm boundary around the mind.

Step 3 — The Final Sentence

Speak softly:

"My sleep is protected. My mind is calm."

This seals the night.

---

4) Weekly Strengthening (One Day Extra Power)

Once per week, strengthen the grid.

On that day:

- keep the lamp burning longer (10–15 minutes)
- repeat mantra for 10 minutes
- offer a simple prayer for home peace and protection

This strengthens the grid like reinforcing a fortress wall.

---

5) The Home Protection Grid Rules (Strict and Powerful)

To keep the method exceptional, follow these rules:

- keep the prayer corner fixed
- keep the lamp discipline daily
- keep the mantra fixed
- avoid clutter and unnecessary noise
- maintain weekly strengthening

This makes the home a permanent stability zone.

---

6) Signs the Grid Has Activated

Within days of consistent practice, the seeker may notice:

- the home feels calmer
- sleep becomes deeper
- fewer unnecessary arguments
- better morning clarity

- reduced mental heaviness
- increased confidence and peace

These are the signs that the grid is alive.

---

7) Mystic Secret: A Home Can Become a Spiritual Armor

When a home is charged daily with light and mantra, it becomes more than a place.

It becomes a guardian field.

The seeker begins to experience something extraordinary:

even when the outer world is intense, the inner world remains stable—because the home itself is protecting the mind.

This is why the Home Protection Grid is so powerful.

It does not wait for problems.

It builds protection before the world touches you.

---

8) Closing Insight: The Home Becomes the Shield of Destiny

Kaal Sarp Dosha becomes easier to stabilize when the home becomes stable.

Because the seeker returns to a calm field daily.

And the final truth of this chapter is luminous:

When the home becomes a temple of discipline,

destiny becomes lighter—

and protection becomes permanent.

Chapter 24 — The 30-Day Reset

The Complete Program That Rewrites the Inner Rhythm and Seals Destiny Stability

A true reset is not rest.

It is reprogramming.

It is the moment the seeker stops moving in scattered patterns and begins moving in **disciplined alignment**—so the Rahu–Ketu corridor loses its power to disturb, and gains its higher function: protection, clarity, and spiritual strength.

This chapter is the strongest practical chapter in the entire Remedy Vault.

Because it gives the reader a complete 30-day system—simple enough to follow, powerful enough to feel extraordinary, and structured enough to produce real results in daily life. It is not a collection of random remedies. It is a single designed program that activates stability like a mechanism.

This is the promise of the 30-Day Reset:

When discipline becomes continuous, the axis becomes obedient.

And when the axis becomes obedient, destiny becomes smooth.

The 30-Day Reset Program

One System. One Rhythm. One Transformation.

The Rules (Strict, Simple, Unbreakable)

For 30 days, follow these rules without compromise:

1. **One mantra only** — *Om Namah Shivaya*
2. **One time daily** — fixed practice time
3. **No break in practice** — continuity is the power
4. **Lamp daily** — steady flame, steady mind
5. **Charity once weekly** — karma purification
6. **Temple once weekly** — field correction
7. **Sleep discipline** — the night must become sacred

This program is designed to be realistic and executable.

The strength is in repetition, not complexity.

Daily Core Practice (12 Minutes)

(Do this every day for 30 days)

This is the daily engine of the reset.

Step 1 — Water Seal (1 minute)

Sip water in 3 sips with inner command:

- "My mind is calm."
- "My path is protected."
- "My destiny is stable."

Step 2 — Breath Lock (2 minutes)

Slow breathing. Exhale longer than inhale.

Step 3 — Mantra Bandhana (6 minutes)

Repeat: **Om Namah Shivaya**

Slow, steady, rhythmic.

Step 4 — Lamp Gaze (2 minutes)

Look at the flame calmly.

Step 5 — One-Line Seal (1 minute)

Speak aloud:

"Today I walk in discipline, and discipline protects me."

This completes the daily reset circuit.

Week-by-Week Activation

Each week upgrades the power level

Week 1 (Days 1–7): The Foundation Lock

Goal: Build continuity and rhythm.

Add these actions:

- keep practice at the same time daily
- reduce unnecessary distractions
- maintain calm speech discipline

Inner result: the mind begins to settle faster.

Week 2 (Days 8–14): The Shield Activation

Goal: Strengthen protection and decision clarity.

Add these actions:

- apply the **3-breath rule** before important decisions
- avoid rushed spending and rushed commitments
- keep the lamp burning 10 minutes once in this week

Inner result: clarity becomes sharper.

Week 3 (Days 15–21): The Corridor Correction

Goal: Purify karmic pressure and strengthen stability.

Add these actions:

- charity once in this week (food or support)
- temple circuit once in this week
- increase mantra time by 2 minutes if possible

Inner result: life flow becomes smoother.

Week 4 (Days 22–30): The Destiny Seal

Goal: Lock stability into the system permanently.

Add these actions:

- keep silence 3 minutes daily after mantra
- avoid negative speech and unnecessary arguments
- protect sleep discipline strictly
- repeat the one-line seal morning and night

Inner result: stability becomes natural.

Weekly Mandatory Practices (Very Powerful)

1) Charity Key (Once per Week)

Give food, support, or donation quietly.

Seal with one line:

"May this act purify my destiny and protect my path."

2) Temple Circuit (Once per Week)

Follow Chapter 22 method exactly.

The Night Seal (Daily — 3 Minutes)

This is the secret protection layer

Before sleep:

1. Repeat **Om Namah Shivaya** *(27 times)*
2. Speak softly: **"My sleep is protected. My mind is calm."**

This seals the dream field and stabilizes the corridor deeply.

The Three Signs the Reset Has Worked

By Day 30, the seeker should notice:

1. **calmer mind and cleaner decisions**
2. **reduced inner pressure and improved sleep**
3. **smoother progress and stronger confidence**

These are not imagination.

These are stability signatures.

What to Do After Day 30

Make it permanent without effort

After completion, continue with:

- daily 6-minute mantra
- daily lamp (2 minutes)
- weekly charity
- weekly temple circuit

This becomes the permanent shield.

Closing Seal: The Reset Becomes a New Destiny Rhythm

The 30-Day Reset is not a temporary practice.

It is a reconfiguration of the inner command system.

When the seeker completes it sincerely, the Rahu–Ketu corridor becomes organized. The mind becomes stable. The path becomes protected.

And the final truth of this chapter is luminous:

When discipline becomes continuous,

Kaal Sarp Dosha becomes silent—

and destiny becomes luminous.

Chapter 25 — The Final Seal

The Last Lock That Makes Protection Permanent

There comes a moment in every sacred practice when effort stops feeling like effort.

The discipline becomes natural.

The mind becomes steady.

And the seeker realizes something extraordinary:

the corridor has changed.

Not because the horoscope disappeared—

but because the seeker's inner command has become stronger than the horoscope's pressure.

This chapter is the completion chamber of the Remedy Vault.

It is the final lock. The closing seal. The point where remedies stop being "things you do" and become **the way you live**—quietly, powerfully, permanently.

In Jyotisha, a remedy becomes unstoppable only when it reaches this stage:

it becomes identity.

This chapter teaches the reader how to seal the transformation so deeply that stability remains, clarity remains, and protection remains—without struggle.

Because the greatest victory over Kaal Sarp Dosha is not dramatic change.

It is **unbreakable steadiness.**

1) What the Final Seal Truly Is

The Final Seal is not a new ritual.

It is the completion of a system.

It is the moment when the seeker locks three forces into one rhythm:

1. **Mind Stability**
2. **Speech Purity**
3. **Action Discipline**

When these three become consistent, the Rahu–Ketu corridor becomes cooperative. Life becomes smoother. Decisions become clean. Inner pressure becomes silent.

This is the final truth:

Kaal Sarp Dosha loses power when the seeker gains command.

2) The Three Seals of Permanent Protection

This chapter is built around three seals.

They are simple, yet absolute in power.

Seal 1 — The Morning Seal (5 Minutes)

Every morning, do this without fail:

- 1 minute water sip seal
- 2 minutes slow breath
- 2 minutes mantra: **Om Namah Shivaya**

Then speak one sentence:

"My mind is steady. My path is protected."

This is the daily lock.

Seal 2 — The Speech Seal (All Day Discipline)

This is the most underestimated remedy in Jyotisha.

Speech is destiny's switch.

For Kaal Sarp mastery, keep this rule:

Speak slowly. Speak clearly. Speak only what is necessary.

Avoid:

- emotional reactions
- unnecessary arguments
- rushed promises

This does not weaken the seeker.

This strengthens the seeker.

Because when speech becomes pure, karma becomes clean.

Seal 3 — The Night Seal (3 Minutes)

Before sleep, repeat:

Om Namah Shivaya *(27 times)*

Then speak softly:

"My sleep is protected. My mind is calm."

This seal is exceptionally powerful because it protects:

- the dream field
- the subconscious rhythm
- the next day's mental clarity

Night discipline is destiny discipline.

---

3) The Final Seal Method (Once Per Month)

The Master Reinforcement

Once every month, perform this special reinforcement:

1. Visit a temple (Temple Circuit)
2. Light a lamp at home after returning
3. Do 108 repetitions of mantra
4. Give one charity act quietly

This monthly reinforcement strengthens the entire remedy system like a final tightening of a sacred knot.

It creates a powerful result:

protection becomes permanent.

---

4) The Proof of Completion: The Five Signs of Mastery

When the Final Seal has activated fully, the seeker experiences these five signs:

1. **clarity becomes natural**
2. **sleep becomes deeper and calmer**
3. **decisions become faster and wiser**
4. **emotional pressure reduces sharply**
5. **life flow becomes smoother and more guided**

These are the signatures of victory.

Not victory over life—

victory within life.

---

5) The Secret of Permanent Results

The reader must remember the ultimate secret:

Remedies work best when they become small and permanent.

Many people seek dramatic rituals.

But the Rahu–Ketu corridor obeys steady rhythm.

This is why the Final Seal is so strong.

It is small enough to be maintained forever.

And what can be maintained forever becomes destiny itself.

---

6) What to Do If a Day Is Missed

The Final Seal is strong and forgiving.

If one day is missed:

- do not panic
- do not feel guilt
- restart immediately the next day
- add one extra mantra cycle

The corridor respects return.

Return is strength.

---

7) Mystic Completion: The Seeker Becomes the Remedy

This is the highest stage.

At first, the seeker performs remedies.

Later, the seeker becomes stable through remedies.

Finally, the seeker becomes the remedy itself.

The mind becomes a lamp.

The speech becomes a mantra.

The daily life becomes a temple circuit.

And then something extraordinary happens:

the horoscope becomes a guide, not a pressure.

---

8) Closing Seal: The Corridor Becomes Light

This is the final message of the Remedy Vault:

Kaal Sarp Dosha is not a prison.

It is a corridor of transformation.

And transformation becomes a blessing when the seeker walks with discipline.

The Final Seal completes the journey with one luminous truth:

When discipline becomes permanent,

protection becomes permanent—

and destiny becomes luminous.

Conclusion

The Corridor of Shadows Becomes a Path of Light

You have now completed a rare journey—one that is not only about understanding Kaal Sarp Dosha, but about mastering it with clarity, discipline, and strength.

This book was written with one purpose: to replace confusion with structure, and uncertainty with method. Because Kaal Sarp Dosha is not a mystery meant to weaken the seeker. It is a formation that reveals a powerful karmic corridor—one that can be stabilized, purified, and transformed through intelligent practice.

The greatest truth you have gained is simple and exceptional:

The horoscope shows the corridor.

But discipline becomes the key.

When you apply the methods given in this book, you do not merely perform remedies—you activate a system. And when a system becomes consistent, the Rahu-Ketu axis begins to obey rhythm. The mind becomes steady. The path becomes protected. Life begins to move with a smoother order.

Kaal Sarp Dosha is often spoken about as if it is only pressure.

This book has revealed its higher reality:

It is **training.**

It is **refinement.**

It is **destiny's discipline school**—designed to build a seeker who can hold success, peace, prosperity, and spiritual strength without collapse.

The moment you begin steady practice, the corridor changes its expression.

What once felt heavy becomes manageable.

What once felt uncertain becomes measurable.

What once felt like shadow becomes a direction toward light.

Because the final victory is not dramatic.

The final victory is permanent stability.

Final Message to the Reader

The Seal of Mastery

Remember this always:

You do not need many remedies.

You need **one method done daily**.

A small practice performed without break is stronger than a large practice performed rarely. This is the hidden secret of Rahu–Ketu mastery. The nodes do not respond to emotion. They respond to rhythm. And rhythm becomes protection.

If your mind becomes steady, your destiny becomes steady.

If your speech becomes pure, your karma becomes clean.

If your routine becomes disciplined, your path becomes guarded.

You have now received the map, the measurement, the symptom knowledge, and the remedy vault. What remains is the simplest, most powerful act:

practice.

Not with fear.

With confidence.

Not with doubt.

With discipline.

Not occasionally.

Daily.

When you do this, something extraordinary begins to happen:

your life starts to feel protected from within.

And this is the final truth of this book:

Kaal Sarp Dosha becomes silent

in the presence of steady mastery.

May your mind remain calm.

May your path remain clear.

May your destiny remain protected.

Practical Quick Checklist (1-Page)

Kaal Sarp Dosha Mastery — Daily, Weekly, Monthly

◈ Daily (Non-Negotiable Core)

☐ Water Seal (1 minute)

- Sip water in 3 sips with inner command:

- "My mind is calm."
- "My path is protected."
- "My destiny is stable."

☐ **Breath Lock (2 minutes)**

- Slow breathing, exhale longer than inhale.

☐ **Mantra Discipline (6 minutes)**

- **Om Namah Shivaya** *(steady rhythm, one mantra only)*

☐ **Lamp Discipline (2 minutes)**

- Light a lamp and gaze calmly at the flame.

☐ **One-Line Seal (1 minute)**

- "Today I walk in discipline, and discipline protects me."

☐ **Night Seal (3 minutes)**

- **Om Namah Shivaya — 27 times**
- "My sleep is protected. My mind is calm."

◈ Weekly (Protection Multiplier)

☐ **Charity Key (once weekly)**

- Food / support / donation given quietly
- Seal line: "May this act purify my destiny and protect my path."

☐ **Temple Circuit (once weekly)**

- Enter in silence
- 1–3 pradakshina (clockwise)
- Offer prayer + offering
- Sit in stillness 3–5 minutes
- Exit seal: "The protection remains with me."

☐ **Home Protection Grid Strengthening (once weekly)**

- Lamp 10–15 minutes
- Extra mantra time (10 minutes)

◈ Monthly (Master Reinforcement)

☐ **One monthly temple visit + 108 mantra repetitions**

☐ **One meaningful charity act**

☐ **One deep silence practice (10 minutes)**

◈ The Three Master Rules

✔ **One mantra only**

✔ **Same time daily**

✔ **No break in rhythm**

Final Seal Line (Repeat Anytime)

"My mind is steady. My path is protected. My destiny is luminous."

Author's Final Note

A Signature Message to the Reader

Dear Reader,

This book was written for one purpose: **to give you strength.**

Kaal Sarp Dosha is often discussed with excessive mystery and scattered opinions. But the tradition of Jyotisha is not meant to create confusion. It is meant to create **clarity, stability, and progress** through correct understanding and correct practice.

If you have read this book fully, you now hold something rare:

- the logic behind the formation
- the method to measure its intensity
- the ability to recognize its patterns in real life
- and most importantly, the remedy system that stabilizes it permanently

This is not ordinary knowledge. It is a practical spiritual skill.

Remember always: the horoscope is not a cage.

It is a map.

And the seeker is never powerless.

The seeker becomes powerful the moment discipline becomes consistent.

Even a small daily practice—performed without break—can create a transformation so steady and so real that you will feel it in your mind, your sleep, your decisions, and your life direction.

I encourage you to keep the method simple and permanent.

One mantra. One lamp. One rhythm. One steady path.

And when you practice, do not practice with fear.

Practice with confidence.

Because the final truth is luminous:

Kaal Sarp Dosha becomes silent

in the presence of steady mastery.

May your mind remain calm.

May your path remain clear.

May your destiny remain protected.

With blessings and respect,

Dr. Narayanan Namboodiri

Books in this Series

Astrology Remedies & Solutions series is designed for readers who want more than predictions—they want practical solutions rooted in authentic Vedic astrology (Jyotisha). Each book in this collection focuses on one planetary force and explains, in a structured and easy-to-follow format, how that planet influences real-life areas such as career, finance, relationships, health, confidence, and mental stability. With clear explanations, disciplined routines, traditional remedies, and chart-based guidance, this series helps you build a strong foundation for long-term progress—step by step, planet by planet.

Our Books in This Series:

1. **Shani Remedies & Sade Sati Solutions**

This book presents Saturn as the great teacher of discipline, responsibility, and long-term protection. It explains Sade Sati and Shani influence in a structured way and offers practical remedies that strengthen patience, stability, and karmic balance. Readers gain a clear path to turn delays into lasting progress.

1. **Rahu Remedies & Shadow Cleansing**

This book explores Rahu as the force behind intense mental patterns and sudden life shifts, guiding the reader toward clarity and self-mastery. It introduces shadow cleansing as a complete remedy system, including ritual, mantra, temple methods, and Rahasya Yoga. Readers learn how to transform Rahu intensity into focus, confidence, and inner protection.

1. **Ketu Remedies**

This book explains Ketu as the planet of detachment, inner searching, and silent spiritual intelligence. It offers remedies that rebuild focus, strengthen life direction, and support a balanced relationship with solitude and simplicity. Readers gain practical guidance to turn spiritual blocks into spiritual strength.

1. **Kaal Sarp Dosha: Truth, Symptoms & Remedies**

This book presents a realistic and mature understanding of Kaal Sarp Dosha, separating myth from meaningful diagnosis. It explains symptoms through Jyotisha logic and offers practical remedies that support stability, confidence, and steady life improvement. Readers receive clear corrective methods without confusion.

1. **Marriage Delay Remedies (Vedic Guidance)**

This book provides structured guidance on marriage timing through the 7th house, Venus, Jupiter, and dasha analysis. It explains how delays can be understood through horoscope patterns and corrected through refined remedies and lifestyle discipline. Readers gain clarity, confidence, and a stable path toward marriage harmony.

1. **Venus Remedies for Love & Relationship Harmony**

This book reveals Venus as the energy of attraction, romance, beauty, and emotional peace in relationships. It offers remedies that strengthen love, improve harmony in marriage, and refine personal charm through inner balance. Readers learn how to awaken Venus energy with dignity and stability.

1. **Jupiter Remedies for Blessings & Marriage**

This book presents Jupiter as the source of grace, wisdom, family support, and auspicious marriage connections. It offers remedies that strengthen blessings, improve relationship maturity, and support children and family happiness. Readers gain practical methods to build a life guided by protection and good fortune.

1. **Career Growth Remedies (Job + Promotion)**

This book explains career progress through the roles of Mercury, Sun, and Saturn, combining horoscope understanding with practical action steps. It offers remedies that improve confidence, communication, authority, and professional discipline. Readers gain a clear plan for growth, promotion, and recognition.

1. **Money & Debt Remedies (Financial Stability)**

This book focuses on building financial strength through Venus, Jupiter, and the power of the 2nd and 11th houses. It offers practical remedies that improve stability, reduce financial pressure, and strengthen prosperity habits. Readers learn structured methods to grow income and protect wealth.

1. **Protection Remedies (Evil Eye + Negative Energy)**

This book provides a complete system for spiritual safety, home energy cleansing, and mental peace through traditional Vedic methods. It explains protection remedies in a practical and disciplined way, including mantra, rituals, and daily spiritual hygiene. Readers gain calm confidence, strong boundaries, and a protected inner atmosphere.

Also by Dr.Narayanan Namboodiri

Astrology Remedies & Solutions
KAAL SARP DOSHA: Truth, Symptoms & Remedies

Astrology Research & Analysis
Nakshatra Life Guide
Nakshatrakālam 2026
2026 to 2126 Birth Star Wise Analysis

About the Author

Dr. Narayanan Namboodiri is a research scholar in Vedic astrology and a respected author known for his clear, practical, and realistic approach to Jyotish. His work focuses on Nakshatra-based analysis, karmic patterns, and traditional remedies, helping readers understand life with clarity, confidence, and purpose.

www.ingramcontent.com/pod-product-compliance
Lightning Source LLC
LaVergne TN
LVHW090400210926
848480LV00002B/410